GUIDELINES

PESACH

GUIDELINES

More Than Five Hundred
of the Most Commonly
Asked Questions about
PESACH

Rabbi Elozor Barclay
Rabbi Yitzchok Jaeger

TARGUM/FELDHEIM

First published 2002
Copyright © 2002 by E. Barclay & Y. Jaeger
ISBN 1-56871-245-6

All rights reserved

No part of this publication may be translated, reproduced, stored in a retrieval system, or transmitted in any form or by any means, electronic, mechanical, photocopying, recording, or otherwise, without prior permission in writing from the copyright holders.

Please address any questions or comments
regarding these notes to the authors:
E. Barclay (02) 583 0914
Y. Jaeger (02) 583 4889
email: jaeger@barak-online.net

By the same authors:
GUIDELINES TO CHANUKAH
GUIDELINES TO THE YOMIM NORAIM
GUIDELINES TO SUCCOS
GUIDELINES TO PURIM

Published by:
Targum Press, Inc.
22700 W. Eleven Mile Rd.
Southfield, MI 48034
E-mail: targum@netvision.net.il
Fax toll free: (888) 298-9992

Distributed by:
Feldheim Publishers
200 Airport Executive Park
Nanuet, NY 10954
www.feldheim.com

Printed in Israel

*Letter of Approbation received from
HaRav Nachman Bulman zt"l for Guidelines for Succos*

Rabbi Nachman Bulman
Yeshivat Ohr Somayach
Beit Knesset Nachliel

רב נחמן בולמן
מנהל רוחני ישיבת אור שמח
רב ק"ק נחליאל נוה יעקב מזרח

בע"ה

יום ו', י"ח תמוז, תשס"ב פה עיה"ק ת"ו

Friday, eighteenth of Tammuz, 5672, the holy city of Yerushalayim.

I was delighted to see the fifth volume of the **Guidelines** series. The questions and answers in **Guidelines** provide a clear and easily understood format and clarify relevant halachic issues.

It is clear from the quality of this work that Rabbi Elozor Barclay and Rabbi Yitzchok Jaeger have invested great amounts of time and effort in their thorough investigation of these dinim. Every answer has been written carefully and thoughtfully, considering both the classic and the most up-to-date halachic authorities. The accurate Hebrew references will certainly be an invaluable aid for any reader who wishes to investigate further.

I highly recommend this book to any person who is truly searching to know the correct conduct.

Signed with admiration,

נחמן בולמן

מנהל רוחני ישיבת אור שמח
רב ק"ק נחליאל נוה יעקב מזרח ביום הנ"ל
ועיני נשואות לשמים להסכמת שוכן במרומים

הרב רפאל צבי ובר
רב דקהילת קמניץ
ונוה יעקב מזרח, ירושלים

י״ט אלול תשס״א
בס״ד

מכתב ברכה

שמחתי לראות קונטרס הלכות בשפה האנגלית שיצא לאור ע״י ידידי הרב ר' אלעזר ברקלי שליט״א והרב ר' יצחק ייגר שליט״א, והנני מכירם ויודעם בהשתדלות לאסוקי שמעתתא אליבא דהלכתא.

והנני מברכם שיקבלו דבריהם בביהמ״ד.

בברכת התורה,

צבי ובר

RABBI ZEV LEFF
Rabbi of Moshav Matisyahu
Rosh Hayeshiva Yeshiva Gedola Matisyahu

בס"ד
ט"ז שבט תשס"ג

It is with great pleasure that I reviewed the manuscript of "**Guidelines**" to Pesach by Rabbi Elozor Barclay שליט"א and Rabbi Yitzchok Jaeger שליט"א.

A siyum – completion – is a very special and joyous occasion. This volume is a siyum and culminates the series of **Guidelines** to the various Yomim Tovim of the year. As in the previous volumes, the laws and customs are presented in a concise, lucid, and organized fashion. The fact that the vastness of the laws of Pesach could be condensed so masterfully into this volume of **Guidelines** is truly impressive. This volume, as well as the entire complete series of Guidelines, will serve as a guide for those who cannot learn these laws from their original sources, and as a valuable aid even to those who can.

May Hashem grant the authors the ability to continue to benefit Klal Yisrael with further works of Torah and mitzvos for many long happy and healthy years.

With Torah blessings,

Rabbi Zev Leff

Rabbi CHAIM P. SCHEINBERG

Rosh Hayeshiva "TORAH ORE"
and Morah Hora'ah of Kiryat Mattersdorf

הרב חיים פינחס שייינברג

ראש ישיבת "תורה אור"
ומורה הוראה דקרית מטרסדורף

בס"ד, חודש שבט, תשס"ג

מכתב ברכה

הנה הביאו לפני קונטרסי הלכות בשפה האנגלית, בעניני המועדים ועוד, אשר חיברום וערכום הרה"ג ר' אלעזר ברקלי שליט"א, והרה"ג ר' יצחק ייגר שליט"א, וכבר התפרסמו הספרים בקרב בני התורה דוברי אנגלית, ונשאו הדברים חן בעיני רבנן.

ואף שאין עיתותי בידי לעבור על הדברים, וזה זמן רב שאיני יוצא בהסכמה לספרים ובפרט לספרים הנוגעים בעניני הלכה, מ"מ כיון שראיתי שגדולי תורה מסכימים עם הדברים על כן ברכתי תלווה אותם שיזכו וחפץ ה' יצלח בידם להוסיף ולחבר חיבורים נוספים בתורה הקדושה, להגדיל תורה בישראל ולהאדירה.

הכו"ח לכבוד התורה

Chaim P. Scheinberg

רחוב פנים מאירות 2, ירושלים, ת.ד. 6979, טל. 1513-537 (02), ישראל
2 Panim Meirot St., Jerusalem, P.O.B. 6979, Tel. (02) 537-1513, Israel

בית המדרש לאסוקי שמעתתא

בס"ד

מכתב ברכה

הנני בא לברך הני תרי צנתרי דדהבא הרב אלעזר ברקלי שליט"א והרב יצחק ייגר שליט"א, ת"ח העמלים לאסוקי שמעתתא אליבא דהילכתא שנים ע"ג שנים ואשר יראתם קודמת לחכמתם, ובאים לזכות את הרבים בהלכה צרופה ומבוררת ליסודותיה ופרטיה, ולהדריך את ישראל המעשה אשר יעשון אשר רבים כבר נהנו מתורתם.

וזכיתי להצטרף למצות זיכוי הרבים והרבצת התורה הנ"ל כאשר עברתי על כל שאלה ותשובה בבירור ובדיוק פרטי ההלכה ולהעיר ולהאיר במקום הנראה, וכל הרואה יווכח בס"ד המיוחדת אשר מה זכו לפרוס את סבכי ההלכה כשמלה לאחר שזכו לאמר על חכמה אחותי את.

והנני בתפילה ובברכה שיזכו שרבים יהנו מתורתם ושיתגלגל על ידיהם ריבוי קיום התורה בעולם, ולזכות בברכת מזכי הרבים ויזהירו כזוהר הרקיע ומצדיקי הרבים ככוכבים לעולם ועד.

החותם בברכת התורה לומדיה ומקיימיה

יצחק קויפמן
מח"ס יבקש תורה ו"ח
ראש כולל לאסוקי שמעתתא, מו"ץ ברמות

בית המדרש לאסוקי שמעתתא - Beis Medrash La'asukai Sh'maisa
רמות פולין 52/10 - ירושלים - Ramot Polin 52/10 - Jerusalem
טל. 2547 586 / 0971 571-2-972 .Tel

Table of Contents

	Page
Foreword	13
Chapter One: The Month of Nissan	15
Chapter Two: Cleaning the House	23
Chapter Three: Preparing the Kitchen	32
Chapter Four: Kashering Utensils	44
Chapter Five: Supervision for Pesach	50
Chapter Six: Products and their Problems	55
Chapter Seven: Kitniyos	60
Chapter Eight: Gebroktz	64
Chapter Nine: Selling Chometz	66
Chapter Ten: Bedikas Chometz	72
Chapter Eleven: Erev Pesach	82
Chapter Twelve: Fast of the First-born	89
Chapter Thirteen: Preparations for the Seder	93
Chapter Fourteen: The Seder	113
Chapter Fifteen: When Pesach is on Sunday	151
Chapter Sixteen: Chometz after Pesach	156
Chapter Seventeen: Chodosh	158
Guide to Chometz items	161
Glossary	163
Index	168
Hebrew Sources	177

Foreword

With praise and thanks to Hashem, we present to the public a second vastly expanded edition of Guidelines to the laws of Pesach.

More than anywhere else, Pesach abounds with many intricate *halachos*, differing customs, and numerous *chumros*. *Rabbonim* the world over are inundated with questions during the weeks before Pesach, and long gone are the days when all we ask are the Four Questions.

Rarely will a written work be a perfect substitute for a one-to-one discussion with a rav. The answer to a query often depends upon various factors that only further questioning can clarify. Even though much thought and effort has been invested in the phrasing and wording used, it is possible that *halachos* may be misunderstood or misconstrued. Accordingly, any doubts that arise should be discussed with one's local rav.

Our primary intent is to guide the reader through the maze of laws and customs that abound during these joyous days, hence the title Guidelines. It is our hope that this book will provide basic information in order to have a happy and kosher Pesach.

We would like to thank a few individuals, whose contribution to this book was of major significance. First and foremost we mourn the tragic loss of the great *posek* and community leader, *HaGaon* Rav Nachman Bulman, zt"l. Rav Bulman was a source of great encouragement when the series of GUIDELINES was launched, and this book is imbued with his invaluable perspective, reliability, and practicality.

Two exceptional *talmidei chachomim* graciously took time from their busy schedules to help turn this book into a reality. Rav Yirmiyahu Kaganoff, *shlita*, *posek* in *Neveh Yaakov*, thoroughly checked the entire manuscript, providing many invaluable comments and insights. His observations have left their impression on every page of the book. We would also like to express our thanks to Rav Yitzchok Kaufman *shlita, Rosh Kollel La'asukei Sh'maisa* and author of the six volume *halachic* work 'Yevakesh Torah'. His keen perception and comprehensive mastery of the topic, provided many valuable changes and additions throughout the entire book.

Thanks are also due to Rabbi Moshe Dombey and all the staff at Targum Press, who have once again demonstrated their professional expertise with the production of this book.

It is our hope that in the merit of keeping the laws of Pesach punctiliously, Hashem will perform miracles and wonders for us and redeem us from exile, as He did for our ancestors in the days of old.

Elozor Barclay   Yitzchok Jaeger
              Yerushalayim, Shevat 5763

Chapter One
The Month of Nissan

1. What is the special significance of the month of Nissan?

The first commandment given to the Jewish nation while still in Egypt was to sanctify the month of Nissan and declare it to be the first month of the year. Although the year begins with Tishrei, the Torah requires us to count the months from Nissan. The Torah calls Nissan חודש האביב - the spring month, and this word אביב alludes to אב י"ב - the head of the twelve months. By counting the months from Nissan, we are constantly reminded of the miracle of the Exodus from Egypt, which occurred in this month. The Sages say that "In Nissan our forefathers were redeemed from Egypt and in Nissan we are destined to experience the final redemption". This Persian word 'Nissan' closely resembles the Hebrew word *nissim*, which means miracles.

2. What is the special significance of *Rosh Chodesh* Nissan?

The first day of the month of Nissan has special glory, and according to the Sages received ten crowns. Among them, this day was chosen by Hashem for the dedication of the Tabernacle in the wilderness and the inauguration of Aharon as high priest. When the first sacrifices were placed on the altar a heavenly fire descended to consume them, and the Divine presence began to rest upon the Jewish people.

3. What are the main changes to prayers during the month of Nissan?

- *Tachanun* is omitted.
- *Tzidkascha* is omitted at Shabbos *mincha*.
- *Kel malei rachamim* is omitted. A person who has *yahrzeit* during Nissan should recite this prayer before *Rosh Chodesh* Nissan.
- *Av harachamim* is omitted on Shabbos mornings until after Pesach.
- *Mizmor lesodah* and *lamnatzeach* are omitted on *erev* Pesach and *chol hamoed*.
- During the first twelve days of Nissan, it is praiseworthy to say the portions of the Torah that describe the offerings of the *nesi'im*. The appropriate section is read each day (*Bamidbar* 7). On the thirteenth day, the following paragraph dealing with the menorah is read. In a few communities, the portion is read publicly from a *sefer* Torah, but the main custom is to read it individually from a *siddur* or *chumash*.

4. May one eat matzo after *Rosh Chodesh* Nissan?

Many people have a custom to refrain from eating matzo from *Rosh Chodesh* until Pesach and some have the custom not to eat it from Purim. Strictly speaking, it is forbidden to eat matzo only on *erev* Pesach (see question 243).

Chapter One - The Month of Nissan

5. May one fast during Nissan?

- Ordinarily, it is forbidden to fast, even if one has *yahrzeit* for a parent.
- A *chosson* and *kallah* should fast on their wedding day, even if it is *Rosh Chodesh* Nissan.
- It is permitted to fast after having a bad dream.
- First-borns fast on *erev* Pesach unless they attend a *seudas mitzvah* (see chapter twelve).

6. May one visit a cemetery during Nissan?

The prevalent custom is to permit visiting a cemetery after *shiva*, *shloshim* or on a *yahrzeit*, but one should refrain from weeping. Some have the custom not to go during the entire month. It is permitted to visit the graves of *tzaddikim*.

7. What is *ma'os chittim* or *kimcha d'pischa*?

There is an ancient custom dating back to the time of the Talmud for communities to collect money to distribute to the poor for their Pesach needs. Originally, the money was used to buy wheat, hence *ma'os chittim* (money for wheat) or flour, hence *kimcha d'pischa* (flour for Pesach). Today the custom is to distribute money, enabling the poor to purchase their Pesach needs. In some communities essential food items are supplied to needy families.

8. Who is required to contribute to this fund?

A person who has been living in the community for thirty days is obligated to contribute, even if he does not intend to reside there permanently. A person who moves to a community with the intention of settling there is obligated immediately.

9. How much should a person give?

Each person should contribute according to his ability. One must remember that matzo and Pesach supplies are much more expensive than regular foods and many poor people may go hungry if not given proper assistance. It would not be an honor to Hashem to recline in happiness at the seder table while the poor lack food to eat. Neglecting to give charity when one is capable is a serious transgression.

10. Which *b'racha* is recited when seeing trees in blossom?

During the month of Nissan it is usual to see trees blossoming. A special *b'racha* is recited only once a year to praise Hashem for rejuvenating the trees that had been bare throughout the winter. It is praiseworthy to make an effort to recite this *b'racha*.

11. What is the text of the *b'racha*?

ברוך אתה ה' א-לוהינו מלך העולם שלא חיסר בעולמו כלום וברא בו בריות טובות ואילנות טובות ליהנות בהם בני אדם.

12. May the *b'racha* be recited over any tree?

No, it may be said only over fruit-bearing trees.

13. May this *b'racha* be recited over a tree that is *orlah*?

For the first three years of a new tree's life, the fruit that it produces is called *orlah* and may not be eaten. In certain cases, the same is true for an old tree that has been replanted. Since the fruits of this tree may not be eaten, one should preferably not recite the *b'racha* over it.

14. May this *b'racha* be recited over a hybrid tree?

If the crossing is done in order to strengthen the tree and there is no noticeable change to the taste or structure of the fruit, one may recite the *b'racha* over it. This is the case with orange and grapefruit trees. Otherwise, it is questionable whether the *b'racha* may be recited over such a tree and one should endeavor to find a different one.

15. May the *b'racha* be recited over a single tree?

Yes, but it is better to recite it over at least two trees together, and some opinions prefer two trees of different species. According to the Kabbala, the mitzvah is enhanced greatly if the *b'racha* is recited over a large number of trees.

16. Must the *b'racha* be recited only during Nissan?

No. The month of Nissan is mentioned since this is the usual time for blossom to appear, but the *b'racha* may be recited any time. This is particularly relevant for communities in the southern hemisphere where blossoms appear at a different time of the year. A person who sees a tree blossoming at a different time of year should recite the *b'racha* only if *tu bi'shvat* passed since he last recited it.

17. May the *b'racha* be recited on Shabbos or Yom Tov?

Yes, but according to some opinions this should be avoided.

18. May the *b'racha* be recited at night?

Yes, as long as the blossom can be seen.

19. May the *b'racha* be recited indoors while looking through a window?

Yes, but it is preferable to recite it outdoors.

20. If a person did not recite the *b'racha* the first time he saw the blossoms, may he recite it the next time?

Ideally, a person should recite the *b'racha* as soon as he sees the blossoms. If he did not do so (e.g. he does not know the *b'racha* by heart and has no *siddur* with him) he may recite it on the next occasion.

21. If all the blossoms have fallen off the tree may one still recite the *b'racha*?

- If he did not see the blossom, he may recite the *b'racha* on the budding fruit.

- If he already saw the blossom but did not recite the *b'racha*, he may not recite it over the budding fruit.
- If the fruit is fully ripe he may not recite the *b'racha* even if this is his first sighting.

22. Should one try to recite the *b'racha* with a *minyan*?

It is an enhancement of the mitzvah to recite the *b'racha* with a *minyan*, or with at least two other people. However, even if a person is alone, he should recite the *b'racha* at his first sighting.

23. Should women try to recite this *b'racha*?

Since this is not considered to be a time-bound mitzvah from which women are ordinarily exempt, it is praiseworthy for them to try to recite it.

24. Why is the Shabbos before Pesach called Shabbos *Hagadol* (The Great Shabbos)?

Among the many reasons given are the following:
- Before the Jewish people left Egypt, they were commanded to take a lamb on the tenth of Nissan in preparation to slaughter it for the *korban* Pesach. Although the Egyptians worshipped the lamb, they looked on helplessly and did not attack the Jews. This miracle is commemorated on the Shabbos before Pesach, since the tenth of Nissan that year was a Shabbos.
- The name is based on the special *haftorah* that is read on this Shabbos. The prophet describes the coming of *Eliyahu Hanavi*, who will announce the final

redemption and the arrival of *Moshiach*. That day is referred to as the 'great and fearful day'.

25. Why does the rav deliver a special sermon on this Shabbos?

It is a custom for the rav of every congregation to deliver a special sermon, called the Shabbos *Hagadol drasha*. The main purpose is to remind people of the most important laws of Pesach, since these are numerous and complex. Nevertheless, it is impossible for the rav to deal with all topics and it is therefore incumbent upon every individual to study the laws of Pesach during the weeks before Pesach (or at least read Guidelines). Ideally, one should begin this study thirty days before Pesach, i.e. on the day of Purim.

26. Why do some people read the Haggadah on this Shabbos?

There is a widespread custom to recite the Haggadah from *avadim hayinu* until *le'chapair al nafshoseinu* after *mincha* on Shabbos *Hagadol*. The reasons for this are:
- The redemption began on Shabbos *Hagadol*.
- To refresh our memories with the text.

Chapter Two
Cleaning the House

Introduction

Cleaning for Pesach is usually associated with an enormous burden of work, exhaustion, and tension, and the atmosphere in the home is rarely one of joy and eager anticipation for the imminent arrival of Yom Tov. The reason for this tragic situation is two-fold. Firstly, what was once a simple one or two-roomed dwelling is now a multi-roomed house with numerous appliances, making the sheer volume of work overwhelming. Secondly, many stringencies and customs have been added over the generations by those who wished to go beyond the letter of the law, and many people are unable to distinguish between what is essential and what is not. Cleaning the house is a mitzvah, and therefore it should be approached with the same calm and pleasure as any other mitzvah. In order to achieve this goal, it is important to know what is required in order to make the house *halachically* clean for Pesach.

27. Why do we have to clean for Pesach?

There are two different mitzvos regarding the owning of chometz:

- בל יראה ובל ימצא - chometz must not be seen or found in one's possession.
- תשביתו - to dispose of chometz.

According to Torah law, it suffices to destroy the chometz **or** to declare it null and void. However, the Sages required that both should be done because of concern that:
- the declaration may not be totally sincere,
- the chometz may inadvertently be eaten,
- some chometz may be overlooked and not destroyed.

28. Must every crumb of chometz be removed?

The minimum size piece of chometz that must be removed depends on its condition.
- If the chometz is dirty, then only a piece that is the size of a *kezayis* must be removed.
- If the chometz is edible, then even a smaller piece that one may be tempted to eat must be removed. [There is another opinion that even crumbs must be removed.]

Therefore, when cleaning for Pesach, one must remove small pieces of edible chometz or large pieces of inedible chometz. According to the strict letter of the law, one does not have to remove the last crumb from every corner of the house. Nevertheless, the widespread custom is to be meticulous and try to remove every speck of chometz, **provided one has the time and energy to do so**.

29. Should heavy furniture or appliances be moved in order to clean underneath?

There is no need to remove chometz from inaccessible places, e.g. under heavy objects such as the fridge, or behind a radiator. Since all chometz is declared null and void, the main reason for removing it from the house is in order not to inadvertently eat it. Since any chometz that is under such heavy objects will not suddenly become available for eating, the declaration is sufficient. [Some are more stringent and either move the furniture and clean there, or spray underneath with bleach, which has the effect of destroying any chometz that might be there.]

30. Must all the books be checked for chometz?

There is no need to check books. However, since books may contain crumbs, the custom is not to bring any books to the table unless they are new, or have been thoroughly cleaned and checked, or are used only on Pesach. The bookcase should be checked behind and between the books, where children could reach.

31. What about *benshers* and *zemiros* books?

Since these often contain crumbs and are difficult to clean, they should be put away with the chometz dishes and not used during Pesach. [Some are stringent to remove every crumb from them.]

32. Must all the toys be cleaned?

Toys that will be used on Pesach should be cleaned by soaking in soapy water and then checked over. Toys that will not be used on Pesach should be put away. It is a good idea to have toys specifically for Pesach.

33. Must one thoroughly check every item of clothing in the house?

No. This can be avoided by sorting all the clothes into two groups; those that will or may be worn during Pesach, and those that will not be worn.

- Clothes that will or may be worn should be completely free of all chometz. They should be thoroughly checked and brushed out, especially in the pockets and hems. Alternatively, these clothes can be laundered or dry-cleaned. If the clothes are laundered, the pockets should first be turned inside out.
- Clothes that will not be worn require only a quick check to ensure that they do not contain any pieces of chometz. Since they are not going to be worn, there is no concern that one may eat any crumbs that are there. Small crumbs do not have to be removed since there is no prohibition to own them during Pesach. If this is also difficult, one may put away some of the clothes without checking and include them in the sale of chometz (see question 174). [Some are more stringent about crumbs, see question 28].

34. How should the dining room table be cleaned?

This requires a thorough cleaning. It should be meticulously checked between the leaves, on any lips or shelves, the legs etc.

35. Should the dining room table also be covered?

In addition to cleaning the table, the custom is to cover it with a covering that is waterproof (such as plastic). This material should be thick enough that it will not tear during Pesach.

36. How should the chairs be cleaned?

It is advisable to wash the chairs, if possible, or brush them well. Efforts should be made to remove any crumbs that are trapped in the crevices.

37. Does the couch have to be washed?

There is no need to wash the couch. It should be brushed or vacuumed to remove any chometz. If the cushions are removable, they should be removed first.

38. Do light switches and door handles have to be cleaned?

Household appliances that are used during the year and on Pesach need to be checked (and cleaned when necessary). This includes light switches, handles of doors, closets and drawers, phones etc. A phone cord that may have been pulled over the kitchen table should be cleaned thoroughly.

39. How should a child's high chair be cleaned?

It should be cleaned thoroughly, paying particular attention to crevices and joins, where crumbs are usually lodged. If possible, it should be dismantled to facilitate the cleaning. Its table should be covered with a thick waterproof cover and tied or taped down.

40. How thoroughly must a carpet be cleaned?

It is sufficient to vacuum it, since any remaining crumbs are not fit for eating. It does not need to be washed or shampooed. [Some are stringent to roll it up and put it away wherever feasible.]

41. How well must a tiled floor be cleaned?

It is sufficient to wash it with floor cleaner that will spoil any remaining crumbs. There is no requirement to clean between the tiles. Nevertheless, since the floor can never be guaranteed to be completely free of chometz, one should take the following precautions on Pesach (these precautions also apply to a carpeted floor):

- Food or pots should not be placed directly on the floor.
- Silverware that falls on the floor should be rinsed.
- Food that falls on the floor should be rinsed. If it cannot be rinsed it may be eaten, but some have the custom not to eat such food until after Pesach.

42. Are separate tablecloths and dishtowels required for Pesach?

- The widespread custom is to use separate ones. If this is difficult, regular tablecloths and dishtowels may be laundered and used on Pesach.
- Opinions differ whether one may launder terylene tablecloths.

- Plastic tablecloths used for chometz may not be used.

43. How should rings be cleaned?
- Rings that are worn when kneading dough and are not smooth should preferably be put away and not worn on Pesach. If a woman wishes to wear such a ring, it must be cleaned very thoroughly.
- Other rings should be cleaned thoroughly and may be worn on Pesach.

[In addition, some have the custom to pour boiling water over all rings.] Care should be taken to keep them away from chometz after they have been cleaned.

44. How should dental apparatus be cleaned?
- According to some opinions, dental apparatus does not require kashering and a thorough cleaning is sufficient. This includes false teeth, bite plates, retainers, and braces.
- According to other opinions, dental apparatus that is removable should be kashered. It should not be used with hot chometz for twenty-four hours and then boiling water should be poured over it. If one is afraid that this may cause damage, it should be soaked in hot water. If it is not removable, hot chometz should be not eaten for twenty-four hours before the latest time for eating chometz on *erev* Pesach. According to some opinions, this also applies to anyone who has a filling.

45. Is it necessary to wash the doors or walls?

This is unnecessary, but if one wishes to do so, care should be taken that *mezuzos* do not become wet.

46. How should a broom be cleaned?

A broom does not need to be cleaned. Some have the custom to wash it with soapy water or to replace the broom head for Pesach.

47. What other points should be remembered when cleaning for Pesach?

The following is a suggested list of items and places where chometz may be found, some of which may be easily overlooked.

Arts and crafts supplies (may contain noodles, barley etc.), baby carriage, baking utensils, basement, *benschers*, bird cage, bird food, briefcase, car (especially glove compartment and trunk), cook books, crib, fish food, garbage cans, handbags, high chair, knapsack, medicine box, office, pet food, playpen, porch, school bags, shopping bags, storage room, stroller, suitcases, *tallis* bag, toy box, *zemiros* books.

48. How should a person clean a house that he will not be in during Pesach?

- A person who does not want to sell food that is definitely chometz (see question 165) should remove pieces of chometz from the house (see question 28). If the departure date is after Purim, a search for chometz must be made on the evening before departure, but a *b'racha* is made only if the search is done on the night of the fourteenth of Nissan (see question 219). The standard sale of chometz should also be arranged before leaving.

- A person who has the custom to sell food that is definitely chometz does not need to do any cleaning. Instead, he should arrange a special sale of chometz that takes effect before the fourteenth of Nissan. This creates an exemption from searching the house for chometz. [It is preferable for a person who is leaving after Purim to exclude one room from the sale in order to fulfill the mitzvah of *bedikas* chometz in that room. See questions 220 and 221.]
- Regarding different time zones, see question 181.

49. What is the procedure if guests will be using part of the house in one's absence?

This is a complex question and a rav should be consulted.

Chapter Three

Preparing the Kitchen

50. Why must so much effort be put into preparing the kitchen?

In addition to the mitzvos mentioned in question 27, there is a third mitzvah regarding chometz, namely the prohibition to eat it. According to Torah law, one may not eat even the tiniest crumb of chometz. A crumb that falls into food on Pesach will render the food forbidden. It is therefore recommended that the most time and energy be reserved for cleaning the kitchen. It should be totally free of chometz down to the last speck. One can be more lenient with respect to the rest of the house, since it is unlikely that a crumb will find its way from there into any food. (See also question 28.)

51. What are the general principles for making the kitchen kosher for Pesach?

Generally speaking, all items and areas that have been in contact with chometz must be dealt with in one of three ways:
- Kashering.
- Cleaning and putting away.
- Cleaning and covering.

In some cases, cleaning is sufficient and subsequent covering is only a custom.

Chapter Three - Preparing the Kitchen

52. Is there any problem with kashering an oven?

According to some opinions, it is permitted to kasher an oven for Pesach. Others maintain that it cannot be kashered satisfactorily and that it should not be used for Pesach cooking. Accordingly, the oven should be checked for chometz and taped closed. [Ideally, one should follow the second opinion and use a separate oven for Pesach.]

53. According to the lenient opinion, how can an oven be kashered?

The oven should be cleaned thoroughly with an oven cleaner and then not used for twenty-four hours. It should then be switched on to the maximum heat for one hour. The racks that are used during the year may not be used for Pesach cooking and must be replaced. [Even after kashering the oven, cooking should preferably be done only before Pesach. If all six inside walls of the oven are covered with aluminum foil or a metal box insert is used, the oven may be used even during Pesach after it has been kashered.]

54. How can a self-cleaning oven be kashered?

According to most opinions, it is permitted to kasher a self-cleaning oven by running it through the self-cleaning cycle. In such an oven, the racks and the stove grates can be kashered by leaving them inside during this process.

55. Can the grates on the stove be kashered?

No. The grates (that the pots sit on) should be cleaned and completely covered with thick foil. [Some are stringent to use a blowtorch to clean them before covering them with foil.] The more recommended procedure is to use a separate set for Pesach.

56. How can the burners on the stove be kashered?

The burners (the circular metal pieces from which the flames appear) should be cleaned thoroughly, particularly in and around the holes. The gas should then be lit and left on high for 5-10 minutes.

57. How can the stove tray be kashered?

The tray onto which food falls should be cleaned well and covered with thick foil. (It is a good idea to smear vaseline onto the tray to help the foil stick. This will also make the foil easy to remove after Pesach.)

58. How can the second tray be kashered?

Some stoves have a second tray beneath the upper tray, which catches any falling debris. If this tray is easily accessible, it should be cleaned and covered. If the tray is not easily accessible, nothing needs to be done.

59. Does the surface above the stove have to be cleaned?

In the process of cooking during the year, a ventilator or cabinet that is above the stove is regularly hit by chometz steam. This surface should be cleaned and covered with thick foil or plastic. Similarly, the hinged stove cover should be removed and put away, or cleaned and covered. [Many have the custom to cover the wall behind the stove to prevent pots from touching it.]

60. How can an electric stove be kashered?

Electric elements should be kashered by switching on the highest heat for five minutes. The area between the elements should be cleaned and covered.

61. Can an electric hot plate be kashered?

No, but it can be used on Pesach if it is cleaned of visible spills and covered with thick foil. [According to some opinions, boiling water should be poured all over it after it has reached its highest temperature (remembering to unplug it first). It should then be covered.]

62. Can a microwave be kashered?

According to some opinions it can be kashered. It should be cleaned thoroughly and left for twenty-four hours. Then a bowl of water should be boiled inside it for 15-20 minutes. A new glass plate should be obtained or it should be covered. The walls and roof do not need to be covered, but the food should preferably be cooked in closed containers. [According to some opinions, a microwave cannot be kashered.]

63. Can a *blech* be kashered?

No. A separate one must be used.

64. Can a dishwasher be kashered?

There are many difficulties involved with kashering a dishwasher. It should be checked for chometz and taped closed.

65. Can one kasher a Shabbos kettle?

No, this item is difficult to kasher and a separate one should be used for Pesach.

66. Can a steel sink be kashered?

A steel sink can be kashered by pouring boiling water onto it. One must follow these points:
- Nothing hot should be placed directly into the sink for twenty-four hours prior to kashering.
- The sink should be perfectly clean and dry before kashering.
- The sink should be kashered one section at a time. After one section has been kashered, the sink should be wiped dry before kashering the next section. This is to prevent the spreading of water from the kashered area to the non-kashered area, which would cool down the boiling water that is to be used for the next section.
- One should not use a Pesach kettle for the kashering. One should use a regular kettle or a pot that has not been used for hot chometz in the last twenty-four hours.
- The stream of water must be unbroken between the kettle and the sink.

67. Can an enamel sink be kashered?

No. It should be cleaned well, but it is not necessary to pour boiling water onto it. [Some are strict to do so]. Since it is forbidden to put a Pesach pot onto a chometz surface, the bottom of the sink should be covered. This can be done by using an insert, or by covering the bottom of the sink with plastic, wood, foil, or anything else that is waterproof. [Ideally, this covering onto which the Pesach dishes are placed, should be raised off the floor of the sink.] Some cover the sink with contact paper or thick foil.

68. What other precautions should be taken with respect to the sink?

Boiling water should be poured down the drain hole, followed by bleach that will spoil any remaining chometz.

69. What should be done with the sink faucets?

The sink faucets should be cleaned well and boiling water poured over them.

70. Should the sink spout be kashered?

The spout should be kashered since it is often hit by chometz steam and splashes. This can be done by turning on the hot water faucet and letting hot water flow through the spout, while simultaneously pouring boiling water onto it. It is recommended to remove or replace the filter that is screwed onto the spout.

71. May hot water be used in the sink during Pesach?

Yes. [Some have a custom not to do so, unless the sink is kashered or fully covered.]

72. Must one replace the cup that is used for washing one's hands by the sink?

No. It is sufficient to clean it thoroughly.

73. How can the fridge be prepared for Pesach?

A detergent should be used to clean the fridge. This guarantees that any remaining crumbs become unfit for a dog to eat and no longer considered to be chometz. The handle should be cleaned well.

74. What about the rubber seal on the fridge door?

The rubber seal should be cleaned with a Q-tip, toothbrush, or a screwdriver that is covered with a cloth. If it is torn and there are crumbs inside, one should try to get them out. If this is difficult, the tear should be covered or bleach poured in.

75. Should the fridge shelves be covered?

One does not need to cover the shelves if they are clean, but many do. (If the shelves are covered, they should be perforated to allow air to circulate.) If chometz must be kept in the cleaned fridge during the last few days before Pesach, it should be wrapped well in order not to invalidate the entire cleaning.

76. Do the inside walls of the fridge need to be covered?

No.

77. How should the freezer be cleaned?

In the same manner as the fridge.

78. May food that is not kosher for Pesach be stored in the fridge or freezer during Pesach?

The following types of food may be kept in the fridge or freezer during Pesach although they may not be eaten:
- Manufactured foods that are not certified kosher for Pesach, but contain no chometz.
- Pure *kitniyos*.
- Food that was cooked in a chometz pot before Pesach but does not contain any actual chometz.

Such foods should be wrapped well and labeled clearly to ensure that they are not accidentally eaten. Pure *kitniyos* do not need to be wrapped and labeled, but *kitniyos* products do (see questions 154 and 155).

79. If one wishes to sell definite chometz to a non-Jew, may it be kept in the fridge or freezer during Pesach?

- If the fridge or freezer will not be used during Pesach, this is permitted. The fridge or freezer should be taped closed and labeled 'chometz'.
- If the fridge or freezer will be used during Pesach, this should be avoided, since sold chometz must ideally be put away in a place that will not be used

during Pesach. In extenuating circumstances the chometz may be stored in one particular section of the fridge or freezer. It should be wrapped well, sealed, and labeled 'chometz'.

These items should be specified in the sale of chometz.

80. Can mixers and blenders be kashered?

- If flour or chometz was used in the mixer, the blades and bowl cannot be kashered but must be replaced. The rest of the machine must be opened and cleaned thoroughly to prevent flour or chometz being released during use on Pesach.
- If flour or chometz was not used in the mixer, the blades may be kashered. The bowl may also be kashered if it is made of metal, but if it is made of glass or plastic a rav should be consulted (see question 94). The rest of the machine should be cleaned well and covered.
- Since a blender is difficult to clean, the blades and bowl should be replaced. The rest of the machine should be cleaned well and covered.

81. How thoroughly must a toaster be cleaned?

Since this will not be used during Pesach, it is sufficient to remove loose crumbs by shaking well. The toaster should then be put away with the chometz utensils. It is not necessary to dismantle it to remove every crumb (see question 86).

82. How can the kitchen counter be kashered for Pesach?

- Counters that are made of metal, pure marble or pure granite can be kashered by pouring boiling water onto them. One must follow these points:
    - Nothing hot should be placed directly onto the counter for twenty-four hours prior to kashering.
    - The counter should be perfectly clean and dry before kashering.
    - The counter should be kashered one section at a time. After one section has been kashered, the counter should be wiped dry before kashering the next section. This is to prevent the spreading of water from the kashered area to the non-kashered area, which would cool down the boiling water that is to be used for the next section.
    - One should not use a Pesach kettle for the kashering. One should use a regular kettle or a pot that has not been used for hot chometz in the last twenty-four hours.
    - The stream of water must be unbroken between the kettle and the counter.
- If one is afraid that such a procedure may damage the counter, it may not be kashered. It should be treated like counters made of other materials.
- Counters made of other materials should be cleaned well and covered with something waterproof that is strong and will not tear during Pesach. [Some are strict and pour boiling water over the counters before covering.]
- Important note: Standard *shayish* counters in Israel are made from a mixture of materials and cannot be kashered.

83. Must the walls behind the kitchen counters be covered with paper?

There is no obligation to put paper on the walls if they are clean, but some do so. (See question 59 regarding the wall behind the stove.)

84. How should the kitchen cabinets be cleaned?

- The inside of the cabinets that will be used should be cleaned well and checked carefully. [There is no need to cover the shelves, but many people do.]
- Cabinets that will not be used do not need to be cleaned, but should be checked for chometz.

85. Should one clean the underneath of the (upper) kitchen cabinets?

Cabinets that are situated above counters and sinks are sometimes splashed underneath with chometz. These areas should be checked, and cleaned if necessary.

86. If the chometz pots are not being kashered, do they have to be scrubbed clean?

No. The custom of scrubbing pots clean originated when people wanted to kasher them for use during Pesach. [Some have the custom to check the pots for any chometz.] (See question 52 regarding the oven.)

87. How should the chometz pots and dishes be stored during Pesach?

They should be stored in a place that is out of reach, so that they will not be used by mistake. If possible they should be put in a different place from usual, but if this is difficult they may be left in their regular place. In either case, they should be made inaccessible by locking the cabinet, or by tying or taping the cabinet and labeling it chometz (compare question 175).

Chapter Four

Kashering Utensils

88. Is it perfectly acceptable to kasher utensils for Pesach?

Although the Torah and the Sages have given clear instructions how to kasher utensils for Pesach, it is praiseworthy to avoid doing so. This is because many utensils are difficult to clean satisfactorily prior to kashering, and because the kashering process is sometimes not performed properly. It is strongly recommended that one use separate pots, dishes, and silverware etc. for Pesach, especially today when these items are relatively inexpensive. If a person cannot afford to buy new utensils he may rely on the kashering process.

89. Are the rules the same as for kashering *treif* utensils during the year?

No, there are many differences. Some of the rules of Pesach are stricter than during the year and some are more lenient. This chapter concerns kashering for Pesach only. When a utensil becomes *treif* from non-kosher foods or from a milk and meat mix-up, a rav should be consulted.

90. How are utensils kashered for Pesach?

There are two standard methods:
- *Hag'ala* – purging. The utensil is submerged in a pot of boiling water.
- *Libun* – burning. The utensil is heated directly by a fire or blowtorch until it reaches an extremely high temperature.

For most utensils, the first method is sufficient, and this is the standard way to kasher utensils for Pesach. Although certain utensils require the second more severe method, it is rarely performed today, since most utensils will be damaged before they reach the required temperature.

91. Which utensils require *libun*?

Those that are used on the fire without any liquid, e.g. a spit, frying pan, baking pan, stove grates, oven racks.

92. May anyone do the kashering?

Since most people are not fully acquainted with the laws of kashering, it should be performed by (or in the presence of) a Torah scholar. The custom is to take utensils to a communal koshering, where the kashering is done by knowledgeable and experienced people.

93. Which materials may be kashered?

One may kasher utensils made of wood, stone, bone, and all metals (e.g. gold, silver, copper, steel, aluminum).

94. Which materials may not be kashered?

One may not kasher utensils made of glass (including pyrex, duralex etc.), enamel, porcelain, china, and teflon. Opinions differ regarding plastic, rubber, and nylon and a rav should be consulted.

95. How clean must the utensil be?

The utensil must be completely clean. All food particles, dirt, grime, etc. must be removed prior to kashering, otherwise the kashering is not effective. As mentioned above, this is probably the most difficult part of the process, and is the reason why many people do not kasher any utensils for Pesach.

96. May one kasher a utensil made of two attached pieces?

Usually, such a utensil may not be kashered, since chometz may be lodged in the join, and the utensil cannot be thoroughly cleaned. Occasionally it may be kashered, if the join is perfectly smooth without any crevices. A rav should be consulted.

97. Does this also apply to handles?

Yes. Since chometz may be trapped between the utensil and the handle, the handle must be removed and cleaned before kashering. If the handle cannot be removed a rav should be consulted.

98. May all metal utensils be kashered by *hag'ala*?

No. Those that are difficult to clean cannot be kashered. These include a sieve, strainer, grater, and grinder.

99. May one kasher a pressure cooker?

Yes. The pot must be cleaned thoroughly, paying special attention to the valve hole. A rav should be consulted concerning the rubber parts.

100. May one kasher a Shabbos kettle?

No, this item is difficult to kasher and a separate one should be used for Pesach.

101. Does a pot cover need to be kashered?

Yes, because it absorbs chometz steam during cooking (see also question 97).

102. May one continue to use the utensil until it is kashered?

No. The utensil must not be used for at least twenty-four hours prior to kashering.

103. May one kasher several items at once?

Yes, but care must be taken to ensure that the water comes into contact with every part of each item. Therefore, if several pieces of silverware are lowered into the water in a wire basket, one must ensure that no piece touches another. A practical suggestion is to place the empty basket into the water and then throw in each item individually.

104. Does one recite a *b'racha* when kashering?

No. Although the Torah requires the kashering of utensils, one does not fulfill a mitzvah by doing so. The Torah is simply prohibiting the use of these articles until the forbidden taste is removed. In addition, since a person may instead use new utensils that do not require kashering, there is no obligation to remove forbidden taste from these articles.

105. May a child be sent with the utensils for kashering?

A child aged six or seven may be sent, and he is believed to report that the items were kashered.

106. Must one kasher new utensils?

This issue is not relevant to Pesach. According to some opinions, new shining metal pots should be kashered before use throughout the year. This is due to a concern that the fat or oil used to create the shine may be *treif*. According to other opinions, this concern is insignificant, and new pots do not require kashering. Some opinions say that it is sufficient to pour boiling water over the outside of the pot. Where kashering for Pesach is done communally, arrangements are often made for people to kasher new utensils in a separate vat. New utensils and used chometz utensils should preferably not be kashered in the same vat.

107. Does this apply to disposable aluminum pans or aluminum foil?

No. These items are heated to an extremely high temperature upon completion, and all traces of fat or oil are destroyed.

108. After kashering for Pesach, may one change the use of a utensil from meat to milk or vice versa?

During the year, one may not kasher a utensil with the intention of changing its use from meat to milk or vice versa. However, if one needs to kasher it for Pesach, one is subsequently permitted to switch its use.

Chapter Five

Supervision for Pesach

109. Why do simple foods such as salt and sugar need to be supervised for Pesach?

Due to today's technology and advanced methods of food processing, even a seemingly simple item may contain chometz. For example:
- Some forms of salt have additives that are made from wheat starch.
- Confectioners sugar often contains a free-flow agent to ensure that the sugar does not clump. This is usually cornstarch, which is *kitniyos*, and sometimes wheat starch. Regular sugar also requires supervision, to ensure that traces of confectioners sugar are not mixed into it.

110. Why can one sometimes find a reliable *hechsher* on *kitniyos* products?

Close examination of the *hechsher* may reveal that this is for all year round but not for Pesach. If the *hechsher* certifies the food 'Kosher for Pesach', this is only for those who eat *kitniyos* (see chapter seven).

111. Can one rely on 'Kosher for Pesach' stickers that are attached to products?

No. All reliable kashrus organizations insist that the Pesach certification is printed on the actual package. Unfortunately, there is fraudulent use of 'Kosher for

Chapter Five - Supervision for Pesach

Pesach' stickers by manufacturers, retailers, and storeowners.

112. Do dried fruits require supervision?

Yes. Wheat starch or flour may be added to prevent clumping. Additionally, a preservative based on sorbic acid may be used, which is sometimes derived from wheat starch.

113. Do frozen vegetables require supervision?

Yes. The equipment that is used to prepare the vegetables may also be used for chometz products.

114. Do canned fruits require supervision?

Yes. The most common sweetener is corn syrup, which is *kitniyos*.

115. Why is there a custom not to use cloves?

This custom originated because they were once soaked in beer. Although this is not done today, many people abide by this custom.

116. Why do some have the custom not to eat garlic?

The reason for this is not known.

117. Why do some people buy milk and milk products for the entire Pesach before Pesach?

- Vitamins A and D may be added to the milk and these may be derived from chometz or *kitniyos*.

- According to some opinions, if a cow eats chometz then the milk that it produces during the next twenty-four hours may not be eaten on Pesach.

118. Why do some people not eat the peel of fresh fruits and vegetables?

This is a stringent custom based upon a fear that the food may have touched or been sprayed with chometz. Some have the custom to peel the food only if this is not difficult, but according to the strict letter of the law even this is unnecessary. According to some opinions, waxed fruits and vegetables should be peeled on Pesach, since the coating may be chometz or *kitniyos*. (Some opinions recommend that this be done all year round since the coating may be *treif*). One must be careful to remove small scale insects that are often found on orange and lemon rinds.

119. Are there any problems with herbs?

Herbs are dried in ovens that may have been used for chometz.

120. Must eggs be washed before they are eaten?

Eggs that come directly from the farm should be washed in case a particle of chometz chicken feed is stuck to them, but eggs sold commercially are pre-washed and do not require a second washing. Some have the custom to boil eggs in a separate pot even after they have been washed, as an extra precaution. Some buy all their eggs before Pesach in case the chickens are fed with chometz (see question 117). The cardboard trays should also be checked before Pesach to ensure that no chometz feed has fallen into them.

121. What general precautions should be taken when buying food for Pesach?

- If possible, one should shop in a store that no longer sells chometz, or at least keeps the chometz far away from the Pesach foods. Even in such a case, one should check the *hechsher* on each individual item and not rely on the fact that it is found in the Pesach section.
- The checkout counter and scales should be completely clean.
- Shopping trolleys and bags should be completely clean.
- One should not buy Pesach products and chometz at the same time.
- If the Pesach foods are brought home by car, they should be placed in a clean area of the car.
- At home they should be placed in a clean area of the house that is well protected from chometz and children.

122. What should one do with leftover pieces of fruit and vegetables that were cut before Pesach with a clean chometz knife?

- Most fruits and vegetables may be rinsed and eaten on Pesach.
- Sharp fruits and vegetables may not be eaten on Pesach. This includes lemons, onions, garlic, radish, and horseradish. When buying horseradish for Pesach,

one must be sure that it was not cut with a chometz knife.

123. Must one avoid walking past a non-Jewish bakery during Pesach?

It is permitted to look at chometz that is owned by a non-Jew, but it is forbidden to deliberately enjoy the smell of freshly baked chometz, even if it belongs to a non-Jew. However, if a person walks past a non-Jewish bakery, he does not transgress if he unwittingly smells the chometz. According to some opinions, it is preferable to avoid the situation if possible.

Chapter Six

Products and their Problems

124. May one own or eat spoiled chometz?

• Spoiled chometz that a person would not eat but a dog would eat is still considered chometz. One may not eat or own such chometz.

• Chometz that is thoroughly spoiled to the extent that even a dog would not eat it is no longer considered chometz. One may own such chometz but not knowingly eat it (except for medicinal purposes – see questions 129 and 130).

125. May one use thoroughly spoiled chometz?

It is permitted to own and benefit from items that contain chometz if they are inedible to a dog. Therefore, shoe polish, floor cleaner, and laundry detergent can be used on Pesach even if they do not have a *hechsher* and may contain chometz.

126. May thoroughly spoiled chometz be applied onto the body?

Yes. Therefore, it is permitted to use soap, shampoo, and creams, even if they do not have a *hechsher* for Pesach. Some have a custom to be stringent and do not use these items unless they have a *hechsher*.

127. Does pure petroleum jelly (vaseline) require a *hechsher*?
No. This is free of chometz.

128. Do medicinal creams require a *hechsher*?
No. Even those who follow the stricter opinion regarding soaps and creams permit their use for medicinal purposes, even if they contain chometz.

129. Do medicines require a *hechsher*?
Bitter or tasteless tablets, capsules, and liquids may be taken on Pesach, even if they contain chometz. This is considered to be thoroughly spoiled chometz, and may be taken for medicinal purposes. Many people try to obtain a chometz-free equivalent, if this is easily available. Where no alternative is available, it is forbidden to put one's health at risk by refusing to take such medicine.

130. What about pleasant tasting tablets and liquids?
- Tablets that are swallowed without chewing or sucking have the same rule as tasteless medicines.
- Tablets that are chewed or sucked must be supervised for Pesach. The same applies to liquid medicine that is pleasant tasting. This is common with children's medicines.

131. What about eye drops, eardrops, nose drops, and throat sprays?
These are all permitted and do not require a *hechsher*.

132. May vitamins be taken on Pesach?

According to many opinions, vitamins are considered to be food and should be taken only if they are supervised for Pesach. If these are not available, one may be lenient to take regular vitamins only if:
- they are bitter tasting or tasteless **and**
- they are medically prescribed.

133. May cosmetics be used on Pesach?

One may use all cosmetics that are not liquids. Since they are inedible to a dog they are permitted, even if they contain chometz (see question 126). This includes all powders, stick deodorants, eye shadow, mascara, blush, rouge, and lipstick. Some use only cosmetics that are supervised for Pesach.

134. Is a fresh stick of lipstick required?

Many use a fresh stick. Strictly speaking, it is sufficient to clean or remove the top of the old one.

135. May one use a flavored lipstick?

Such lipsticks may not be used unless they are supervised for Pesach.

136. May one use liquid cosmetics, e.g. perfume?

There is much debate about this. The problem concerns certain types of alcohol that may be made from grains, e.g. ethyl alcohol. In addition, some perfumes may contain vitamin E or wheatgerm that is chometz. According to some opinions, this may be ignored since the final product is unfit for eating. Other opinions do not consider this to be thoroughly spoiled chometz, since there are people who will drink it by diluting it or by making other improvements to its taste. Strictly speaking, one may be lenient and use all liquid cosmetics. However, there is a widespread custom to use only products that are supervised for Pesach, and include non-supervised products in the sale of chometz. This applies to perfume, cologne, shaving lotion, mouthwash, spray and roll-on deodorants, and hair spray. Liquid cosmetics that do not contain alcohol, vitamin E or wheatgerm are permitted according to all opinions.

137. May one use air-freshener sprays?
Yes. Even if they contain alcohol they are permitted, since they are not applied to the body.

138. Does toothpaste require a *hechsher*?
Although toothpaste is unfit for eating, the widespread custom is to use only one that is supervised for Pesach.

139. Does soap for dishes require a *hechsher*?
This too is unfit for eating, but the custom is to use only soap that has a *hechsher* for Pesach.

140. Are there any problems with pet food?
Most commercial pet food contains actual chometz and may not be owned or used during Pesach. This includes bird feed and fish food. Pets may be given pure *kitniyos* (see question 143) or any chometz-free food

that they can eat. One should consult with a pet store for advice about suitable alternatives.

141. May one use paperware on Pesach?

Paperware may be used even if it is not supervised for Pesach. This includes plates, cups, baking cases, towels, and napkins. Some people do not use paperware for hot foods or liquids unless they are supervised for Pesach. Non-supervised paperware may certainly be used for cold dry foods and for wiping one's hands or tables.

142. Does plasticware require supervision?

Plasticware does not require any supervision. This includes plates, cups, cutlery, straws, bags, and wrap.

Chapter Seven
Kitniyos

143. What are *kitniyos*?

Kitniyos are certain vegetables that may not be eaten on Pesach according to Ashkenazic custom. The most common ones are alfalfa, aniseed, beans, buckwheat, caraway, chickpeas, coriander, cumin, fennel, fenugreek, flax, lentils, maize, millet, mustard, peas, peanuts, poppy seeds, rice, sesame, soy, sunflower seeds, and tofu. (See question 145 for a list of *kitniyos* derivatives).

144. Why do Ashkenazim not eat *kitniyos* on Pesach?

Although they can never become chometz, the Ashkenazic rabbis enacted a prohibition not to eat *kitniyos* for the following reasons:
- Kernels of grain occasionally become mixed with *kitniyos* and if overlooked would cause the mixture to become chometz.
- Some *kitniyos* can be ground into flour and baked to produce bread. This could lead to confusion between grain-bread and *kitniyos*-bread.
- Poor quality grains sometimes look like *kitniyos* and could be used in error.

145. May *kitniyos* derivatives be eaten?

No. Common examples are bamba, cornflakes, corn flour, corn oil, dextrose, glucose, lecithin, mustard, peanut butter, peanut oil, popcorn, sorbitol, soy oil, starch, and tehina. Margarine, mayonnaise, and salad dressing are usually made from *kitniyos* and must have a *hechsher* for Pesach.

146. May cottonseed oil be used?

- In *chutz la'aretz* the custom is to use cottonseed oil.
- In *Eretz Yisroel* there are different customs and the local custom should be followed.

147. May *kitniyos* be eaten in exceptional circumstances?

A person who is sick or has a limited diet may eat *kitniyos* on Pesach since it is not chometz. Similarly, a child may be fed baby formula or cereal made from *kitniyos*. These items should have a reliable *hechsher* for Pesach.

148. If *kitniyos* must be used, should any types be avoided?

Yes. If possible, rice, millet, and buckwheat should be avoided since they are very similar to grains.

149. Are separate utensils needed when preparing *kitniyos*?

The custom is to use separate utensils for *kitniyos*. They may be washed in the Pesach sink.

150. May one cook *kitniyos* on the Pesach stove?

Yes, but care should be taken that the food does not splash or spill onto other pots and pans, or into other food.

151. What if such splashing does occur?

- If a food of *kitniyos* splashes onto the stove or onto other pots and pans, it is sufficient to wipe it off.
- If it splashes into other food, it should be removed if possible. If it has become completely mixed into the other food, it becomes nullified and the mixture may be eaten.

152. May an Ashkenazi eat at the house of a Sephardi on Pesach if no *kitniyos* are served, but the pots have been used to cook *kitniyos*?

Yes. This is permitted even if the pots were used for *kitniyos* within the last twenty-four hours.

153. May *kitniyos* be eaten on *erev* Pesach?

The custom is not to eat *kitniyos* from the time that chometz may not be eaten. In times of need, one may be lenient all day if the food has a reliable *hechsher* for Pesach.

154. Do *kitniyos* have to be sold before Pesach?

No. Since they are not chometz they do not need to be sold. However, *kitniyos* products that are not supervised for Pesach should be sold, since they may contain other ingredients making them questionable chometz. (A good example is cornflakes that often contain malt, which is chometz.)

155. Do *kitniyos* have to be put away?

Pure *kitniyos* do not need to be put away, since they may be given to animals during Pesach (see question 140), and in exceptional circumstances to children and sick people (see question 147). However, *kitniyos* products that are not supervised for Pesach should be put away with chometz to be sold, since they may not be used during Pesach.

156. May unsupervised *kitniyos* products be stored in the fridge during Pesach?

Yes. They should be wrapped up and labeled to ensure that they are not accidentally eaten. (See also question 78.)

Chapter Eight

Gebroktz

157. What is *gebroktz*?

Literally translated from Yiddish as 'soaked', this refers to matzo or matzo meal that has been soaked or cooked in a liquid.

158. Why do some people have the custom not to eat *gebroktz*?

This is because of a concern that some flour was not kneaded properly into the dough, and this could become chometz if the matzo gets wet.

159. Does this custom have to be followed?

Strictly speaking, *gebroktz* is permitted, but many have the custom not to eat it. Some have a custom to allow other liquids, e.g. pure fruit juice, eggs, oil etc., to mix with matzo, being careful only to ensure that it does not soak in water.

160. May a person deviate from his family custom and eat *gebroktz*?

A person who has a family custom not to eat *gebroktz* must abide by it. In extenuating circumstances, a rav should be consulted.

161. May a person with this custom eat non-*gebroktz* food that has been prepared in pots used for *gebroktz*?

There are different customs about this.

162. If a baby or sick person must eat *gebroktz* or *kitniyos*, which is preferable?

It is preferable to eat *gebroktz* rather than *kitniyos*.

Chapter Nine

Selling Chometz

163. Why was the procedure of selling chometz originally instituted?

Originally, only those who traded in food sold chometz in order to avoid major financial difficulty. It was done personally with a non-Jew and the chometz was taken out of the house. When this became a practical problem, a locked room containing the chometz was sold to the non-Jew (or rented, in *Eretz Yisroel* where it is forbidden to sell land to a non-Jew) and the key was given to him. More recently, many other leniencies have been included.

164. May individuals sell their chometz to a non-Jew?

Due to the highly complex laws of acquisition between Jew and non-Jew, the custom is that the rav sells the chometz for the community.

165. May one sell food that is definitely chometz?

- According to most opinions, one may sell food that is definitely chometz.
- Some have the custom not to sell food that is definitely chometz. This is because the sale involves complex *halachic* issues, and it is difficult to fulfill the requirements in a way that satisfies all opinions. One

may be lenient if disposing of it would cause financial hardship.

166. May one sell food that is questionable chometz?

According to all opinions, one may sell food that is questionable chometz.

167. Aside from bread, which foods are definitely chometz or contain chometz?

Such foods include beer, biscuits, bissli, bran, brewers yeast (nutritional yeast), cake, cereals (that contain one of the five grains), cookies, crackers, dough, drinks from grains (chico), instant quaker oats, macaroni, malt, noodles, oatmeal, puffed wheat, semolina, snack bars (that contain one of the five grains), soup nuts, spaghetti, wafers, wheat germ, whisky, and yeast extracts. [The five grains are wheat, barley, spelt, rye, and oats].

168. May flour be sold?

The custom is to permit the sale of flour. Although some have the custom not to sell food that is definitely chometz (see question 165), flour is not considered to be definite chometz. This is because the grains are washed quickly and probably have not been in contact with water for sufficient time to become chometz.

169. Which products are questionable chometz and may be sold?

Alcohol, alcoholic drinks (except beer and whisky), all canned foods, baked beans, baking powder, burgol (whole wheat), brown sugar, candies, chewing gum, chocolate spread, cocoa, coffee, custard powder, dextrose, dried fruit, drinking chocolate, falafel powder, flavorings, flour, fruit drinks, glucose, granola, grape sugar, instant puddings, pleasant tasting medicines, mustard, pearl barley, pickled meats, pickled vegetables, play-do, powdered soups, raw oats, regular matzo and matzo meal, salted nuts and seeds, sausages, soda, starch, spices, vegetarian meat, vinegar, and vitamins.

170. Should everyone arrange the sale of chometz?

Due to today's technology and advanced methods of food production, even a seemingly simple item may contain chometz (see question 109). Therefore, everyone is advised to arrange the sale of chometz.

171. Do chometz pots and dishes need to be sold?

No. If pots were sold, they would need to be *toiveled* again after Pesach when they are reacquired from the non-Jew. The custom is to include in the sale any chometz that remains in the pots. (See also question 87.)

172. Do dried flower arrangements need to be sold?

Dried flower arrangements that contain one of the five grains should be put away and included in the sale, in case they were in contact with water and may have become chometz.

173. What else should be included in the sale?

If a person owns stocks in a company that deals with chometz, he should preferably list them. According to some opinions, this ownership establishes him as a partial owner of the chometz.

174. Should every item of chometz and its exact location be specified in the contract?

Preferably, the exact location of all the chometz should be specified. However, if an item or a location was omitted, it is included in the sale. This is because there is a clause in the contract that includes all types of chometz in all places.

175. Does one need to lock the place where the chometz is stored?

If possible, yes. Otherwise, it should be taped closed and labeled that there is chometz inside. A section of the house that is being sold should be locked if possible, or closed off (see question 208).

176. If the house will be vacant during Pesach, does this affect the sale?

Since the non-Jew must have access to the chometz, one should leave a key with a neighbor and inform the authorizing rav of its location.

177. During Pesach, may items be taken from sections of the house that have been sold?

The contract gives permission to the seller to retrieve an item from these locations in times of need.

However, one should not do so too often, since this would indicate that the sale has not been taken seriously.

178. May a person appoint an agent to sell chometz with the rav?
Yes. There are suitable contracts of sale available for those who cannot arrange the sale personally.

179. What if a person or his agent cannot personally meet the rav?
Ideally, either the person or his agent should sign a contract in the presence of the rav and grasp an object to strengthen his authorization. However, in extenuating circumstances, a person may arrange the sale with the rav by telephone.

180. Should one pay the rav for his services?
Although this is not strictly required, many people have the custom to do so. According to some opinions, this strengthens the rav's authorization.

181. How should the sale be arranged if one is going to be in a different time zone during Pesach?
He should tell this to the rav who is selling the chometz. The rav will then be able to schedule the sale and repurchase of the chometz in an acceptable way.

182. May a person who lives in a rented house, rent part of it to a non-Jew?

This is allowed even without explicit permission from the owner. This is true even if there is a clause in the rental contract that forbids subletting, since the non-Jew has no intention to live in the house.

Chapter Ten
Bedikas Chometz

183. When should *bedikas* chometz be done?
At nightfall on the evening of the fourteenth of Nissan.

184. What if a person is unable to begin the search at nightfall?
He should begin as soon as possible.

185. When should a man *daven ma'ariv*?
The custom is to *daven ma'ariv* at nightfall and do *bedikas* chometz immediately afterwards.

186. What if a person intends to *daven ma'ariv* later in the evening or missed the *minyan* at nightfall?
According to some opinions, he should do *bedikas* chometz immediately at nightfall. According to others, he should delay searching for chometz until after *davening ma'ariv*. One should make an effort to *daven ma'ariv* immediately at nightfall in order to avoid this situation.

187. What if a person is usually at work at nightfall?
Every effort should be made to start *bedikas* chometz at nightfall. Therefore, a person should leave his place

of work before nightfall in order to do *bedikas* chometz on time.

188. Is there any work restriction before nightfall?

Yes. When a person is involved in various activities he may not notice the passage of time, and may miss the ideal time to do *bedikas* chometz. Therefore, one may not start any new activity within half-an-hour before nightfall. If one began before the half-hour period, one may continue until nightfall. At nightfall, one must stop all activities.

189. What type of activity is forbidden within this half-hour?

All tasks. This includes having a haircut, shaving, and bathing.

190. May one begin to study Torah during this half-hour?

• According to some opinions, it is forbidden to study Torah at home. If he appoints another person to remind him to do *bedikas* chometz on time, he is permitted to study.

• It is permitted to study Torah in shul while waiting for *ma'ariv*.

191. May one eat or drink before *bedikas* chometz?

During the half-hour before nightfall, one may not eat more than a *kebeitza* of bread or cake. There is no restriction on other foods or drinks during this period.

At nightfall, one should begin the search without delay (see also question 185).

192. May one sleep before *bedikas* chometz?
This is certainly forbidden within the half-hour before nightfall, since there is a strong possibility that one may oversleep.

193. Do all these restrictions also apply to women?
These restrictions apply to any person who has to do *bedikas* chometz. Therefore, a woman who lives alone or whose husband is away must keep all the above restrictions.

194. Is a *b'racha* recited over the search?
Before beginning the search one should recite the *b'racha* אשר קדשנו במצותיו וצונו על ביעור חמץ.

195. What if a person forgot to recite the *b'racha*?
The *b'racha* should be recited if the search has not yet been concluded.

196. What if a person finished the entire search without reciting the *b'racha*?
According to some opinions, the *b'racha* may be recited before the chometz is burned on the following day.

197. Must the homeowner himself do the search?

Ideally, yes. If he wishes, he may ask another person to assist in the search, and in extenuating circumstances may even ask another person to do the entire search on his behalf.

198. Should every person who is going to assist in the search recite the *b'racha*?

No. They should listen to the *b'racha* that the homeowner recites and say 'amen'.

199. Who should recite the *b'racha* if the homeowner himself is not participating in the search?

The person who is doing the search should recite the *b'racha*. If possible, the homeowner himself should recite the *b'racha* and search a little.

200. What should one think about before reciting this *b'racha*?

A person should have in mind that he is starting to fulfill the mitzvah to destroy his chometz, and will conclude the mitzvah on the following day.

201. What if a person speaks after reciting the *b'racha* before beginning the search?

It is forbidden to speak after reciting the *b'racha* before beginning the search. A person who speaks must repeat the *b'racha*, unless what he says is connected to the search.

202. What if he speaks about unrelated matters during the search?

The *b'racha* does not need to be repeated. However, in order not to be distracted from the search, one should not speak unnecessarily.

203. Should a person repeat the *b'racha* if he has more than one property to search?

No. He should go without interruption from one place to the other and continue his search there.

204. What if he was unavoidably interrupted between checking two properties?

The *b'racha* should not be repeated.

205. Must one's office be searched on the night of the fourteenth of Nissan?

Ideally, yes. If it is far from the house and it is very inconvenient to travel there on the night of the fourteenth, he should include the office in the sale of chometz (provided he will not be there during *chol hamoed*). Alternatively, he should search the office without a *b'racha* on the previous evening (see also question 219).

206. What should one look for when doing *bedikas* chometz?

Every part of the house must be checked for chometz and it is not sufficient to simply look for the ten pieces of bread (see question 210). Even if many days have already been spent cleaning the house, one must utilize this opportunity to confirm that every part of the house has indeed been thoroughly cleaned and that chometz has not been brought there since (see check-list in question 47). Before the search, one should put out of children's reach all chometz that is to be sold to a non-Jew or that one wishes to eat. Similarly, all chometz found during the search should be put in a safe place until it is burned the next morning.

207. Which parts of the house should be checked?

One must check any area that chometz may have been brought into during the year. Since it is common for small children to carry food around the house, one must check any area that they may have entered.

208. Must one search the areas that are being sold to a non-Jew?

Opinions differ about this, but the main custom is not to search these areas, since any chometz there will in any case be sold to a non-Jew. One may even deliberately avoid checking sections of the house for chometz, and include them in the sale (see also question 175). A person who does not wish to rely on the sale for definite chometz should search these areas for definite chometz.

209. If the whole house has been thoroughly cleaned before Pesach, why is there a search for chometz on the night of the fourteenth?

According to some opinions, one does not need to search a house that clearly contains no chometz. Other opinions require the search in any event. In order to satisfy both opinions, one part of the house should not be cleaned thoroughly beforehand.

210. Why are ten pieces of bread distributed around the house before the search?

In order that the search can be performed with a *b'racha* in a house that is completely clean, the custom is to distribute ten pieces of bread around the house before the search. Whoever puts out the pieces should make a note of where they are located, in case any are not found during the search.

211. What should be the size of these pieces?

Each piece should be less than the size of a *kezayis*. The pieces should be wrapped, to ensure that they do not leave crumbs around the house (see question 28).

212. What should be done if not all the pieces were found during the search?

One is not required to search the house again to find the last piece(s), and one may rely on the declaration that all unseen chometz shall be null and void.

213. May a flashlight be used for the search?

It is perfectly acceptable to use a flashlight, although many maintain their custom and conduct part or all of the search with a wax candle. In places where a person is hesitant to take a candle (e.g. a linen closet), a flashlight must be used.

214. Should the electric lights be turned off during the search?

The lights may be left on since they assist in the search. If they disturb the effectiveness of the candle or flashlight, they should be turned off.

215. When should the first nullification of chometz be said?

This should be said immediately after the search.

216. What if a person forgot to nullify the chometz immediately after the search?

He should say the nullification as soon as he remembers.

217. Must the nullification be said in the original Aramaic?

It is crucial for a person to understand what he is saying and recite it in a familiar language. If he does not understand the Aramaic words, he should say the following declaration in English: **All chometz and leaven that is in my possession that I have not seen, that I have not destroyed, and that I do not know about, shall be null and ownerless like the dust of the earth**. Some have the custom to say the nullification three times.

218. How should *bedikas* chometz be done in a house that will not be used during Pesach?

See question 48.

219. What are the rules of *bedikas* chometz when performed prior to the night of the fourteenth?

If a person or a family leaves the house before the night of the fourteenth, *bedikas* chometz must be performed on the evening before departure. In this situation, all the rules of *bedikas* chometz apply fully (e.g. searching at nightfall, not working or eating beforehand), with two exceptions:
- A *b'racha* is not recited.
- It is not necessary to distribute ten pieces of bread.

The nullification should be said as usual after the search.

220. Is a visitor required to do *bedikas* chometz?

- A visitor is not required to do *bedikas* chometz even if he is given a private room in the host's house. This includes married children who go to their parents for Pesach.
- A visitor is required to do *bedikas* chometz at his own home on the night of the fourteenth. If he goes to his host before the night of the fourteenth, he should do *bedikas* chometz without a *b'racha* on the night before he leaves home (see previous question). If he is selling the entire house to a non-Jew, he is exempt from *bedikas* chometz (see question 208). According to some opinions, one part of the house should not be sold, so that he can fulfill the mitzvah of *bedikas* chometz there.

221. Does a visitor become obligated by paying rent for his room?

- If this is a serious rental agreement (i.e. the owner is not willing to give the room without payment), such a visitor is obligated to do *bedikas* chometz there.
- If this is only a 'token' arrangement in order to artificially create an obligation to do *bedikas* chometz, opinions differ whether it is effective. If such an arrangement is made, the visitor should do *bedikas* chometz in his room, but he should listen to the *b'racha* being recited by the homeowner rather than recite it himself.

222. Are yeshiva and seminary students obligated to do *bedikas* chometz?

Students who live in a yeshiva or seminary are obligated to do *bedikas* chometz in their rooms on the night of the fourteenth with a *b'racha*. If they intend to leave the yeshiva or seminary before the night of the fourteenth, they should do *bedikas* chometz without a *b'racha* on the evening before they leave (see question 219).

Chapter Eleven

Erev Pesach

223. What are the changes to prayers on *erev Pesach*?

One should *daven* early in order to finish eating and burning the chometz by the required time.
- *Mizmor Lesodah* is omitted (by Ashkenazim).
- *Lamnatzeach* is omitted.
- *Kel erech apayim* is omitted if it is a Monday.

224. Until when may one eat chometz?

Chometz may be eaten until the end of the fourth *halachic* hour of the day. There are two ways to calculate this, and the custom is to follow the opinion that reckons the day from dawn until nightfall. The exact time should be found in the local Jewish calendar. After one has finished eating chometz, he should clean his teeth thoroughly.

225. What should be done with the remaining chometz?

It should be destroyed together with the ten pieces of bread that were collected during *bedikas* chometz. The custom is to destroy all the chometz by burning, but if this is too difficult one should burn at least the ten pieces. The remainder of the chometz should first be thrown into a public garbage container. One should remember to empty the domestic garbage bins.

226. Why do some people throw their old lulav into the fire?

Since it was used for one mitzvah, it is fitting to reuse it for another mitzvah.

227. May one pour paraffin onto the fire to increase it?

The custom is to destroy at least one *kezayis* of edible chometz by burning. Since paraffin will spoil the chometz, it may be poured onto most of the chometz (taking the appropriate safety precautions), but not all. Edible oils may certainly be poured onto all the chometz to increase the fire.

228. Must one remain by the fire until all the chometz has been burned?

It is not sufficient for the pieces of chometz to be blackened on the outside, since the inside may still be edible. One must therefore ensure that the chometz is thoroughly burned. If attempts to burn the chometz are failing, one should destroy it by any method, or throw it into a public garbage container.

229. By what time must the chometz be burned?

All the chometz must be burned or destroyed before the end of the fifth *halachic* hour of the day. The exact time should be found in the local Jewish calendar.

230. What if a person cannot make a fire?

The chometz should be disposed of in another way, e.g. by throwing it into a public garbage container or flushing it down the toilet.

231. What should one do after destroying the chometz?

After the chometz has been completely destroyed, one should say the final nullification. If he does not understand the Aramaic words, he should say the following declaration in English: **All chometz and leaven that is in my possession that I have seen and that I have not seen, that I have destroyed and that I have not destroyed, that I know about and that I do not know about, shall be null and ownerless like the dust of the earth**. Some have the custom to say the nullification three times. One should also make a final check in one's pockets to ensure that no crumbs are there.

232. Why is the nullification repeated in the morning?

The nullification that is made at night does not include chometz that is deliberately left or will be bought on the following day. The nullification that is made in the morning includes any remaining chometz that has not been destroyed. It also includes the chometz that is sold to the non-Jew, in the event that something invalidates the sale.

Chapter Eleven - Erev Pesach

233. When is the latest time that one may say the daytime nullification?

It must be said before the end of the fifth *halachic* hour.

234. Who should say this nullification?

Although the evening nullification is said only by the person who does *bedikas* chometz, the morning nullification should be said by everyone who is over the age of bar or bas mitzvah (including married women). This is in case he (or she) owns personal items containing chometz.

235. May one work on *erev* Pesach?

From *halachic* midday one may not do any type of work that is forbidden on *chol hamoed*. The reason is that it is a semi-Yom Tov, being the time that the *korban* Pesach was slaughtered in the Temple. Whoever does forbidden work will see no blessing from it.

236. May one have a haircut or shave?

Yes, but after *halachic* midday it is permitted only when done by a non-Jew.

237. Is it permitted to cut one's nails?

Yes, but one should preferably cut them before *halachic* midday.

238. Is it permitted to launder clothes?

Laundering is forbidden after *halachic* midday. If the washing machine started before that time, it may be left to finish the wash.

239. Is it permitted to put clothes into the dryer?
Yes. This is permitted all day.

240. Is it permitted to iron clothes?
Clothes that are needed for Pesach may be ironed all day.

241. Is it permitted to polish shoes?
Yes. This is permitted all day.

242. Is it permitted to sew?
- It is permitted to make repairs to a garment all day.
- It is forbidden to complete the finishing touches to a new garment after *halachic* midday.

243. May one eat matzo?
It is forbidden to eat matzo on *erev* Pesach (see also question 4). Among the reasons are:
- In order to emphasize the mitzvah of eating matzo in the evening.
- In order to eat the matzo in the evening with appetite.

According to the main custom, one may not eat matzo on the evening of *erev* Pesach (see question 504).

244. May children eat matzo?
Children who are old enough to understand the story of the Exodus should not eat matzo.

Chapter Eleven - Erev Pesach

245. May one eat baked foods containing matzo meal (e.g. Pesach cake)?

According to most opinions, these are also forbidden, since the matzo has not undergone sufficient change.

246. May one eat boiled or fried foods containing matzo meal?

Those who eat *gebroktz* (see chapter eight) may eat such foods (e.g. *kneidlach*), but only until the beginning of the tenth *halachic* hour (halfway between *halachic* noon and sunset).

247. May one eat *kitniyos*?

The custom is not to eat *kitniyos* from the time that chometz may not be eaten. In times of need, one may be lenient all day if the food has a reliable *hechsher* for Pesach.

248. Is there any restriction on other foods?

Foods such as meat, fish, eggs, fruit, and vegetables may be eaten all day. However, from the beginning of the tenth *halachic* hour one should eat with moderation, in order to eat the matzo in the evening with appetite.

249. Is there anything special about *mincha* on *erev* Pesach?

- It is correct to *daven* early (*mincha gedolah*) since in the Temple the afternoon sacrifice was brought earlier than usual to allow time for the *korban* Pesach.
- Following *mincha*, many people have the custom to recite *seder korban Pesach*, which is a collection of

verses from *Tanach* describing the bringing of the *korban* Pesach. We pray that this recital be considered as if we have actually brought the *korban* Pesach.

250. Are men obligated to immerse in a *mikveh*?

In the days of the Temple, men were obligated to purify themselves in a *mikveh* before every Yom Tov. Today, it is not an obligation but a widespread custom. Even if a man does not immerse on *erev* Shabbos, he should make an effort to do so on *erev* Yom Tov.

251. What is the correct time to go the *mikveh*?

After *halachic* midday.

Chapter Twelve
Fast of the First-born

252. When is the fast of the first-born?
First-borns are required to fast on *erev* Pesach. If *erev* Pesach is on Shabbos, the fast is on the previous Thursday.

253. When does the fast begin?
At *halachic* dawn. Although the custom is to attend a *siyum* in shul (see question 259), one must be careful not to have a drink at home before *shacharis*.

254. Why do first-borns fast?
To remember the miracle that they were saved during the tenth plague in Egypt - the slaying of the first-born. The fast ought to have been on the first day of Pesach when the miracle occurred, but since this is Yom Tov the fast was moved a day earlier.

255. Which first-borns are required to fast?
The first-born son of either the father or the mother. The custom is that first-born girls do not fast. A first-born son following a miscarriage (ה"י) is required to fast, as is a first-born son of a Cohen or a Levi.

256. Is a first-born convert required to fast?
Since there is a doubt regarding this case, it is recommended that he attend a *siyum* with the other

first-borns. If he is unable to attend a *siyum*, he does not have to fast.

257. Is a boy born by caesarean section required to fast?

Since there is a doubt regarding this case, it is recommended that he attend a *siyum* with the other first-borns. If he is unable to attend a *siyum*, he does not have to fast.

258. Is a boy below bar mitzvah required to fast?

No, but the father should fast in his place. This applies to a first-born son between the ages of thirty days and bar mitzvah. If the father is himself a first-born, the fast is valid for both himself and his son.

259. What if a first-born finds it difficult to fast?

He is permitted to join a *seudas* mitzvah, such as a *bris*, *pidyon haben* or *siyum*. Since fasting on *erev* Pesach is extremely difficult for anyone, it has become the accepted custom for first-borns to attend a *siyum* and partake of the refreshments served.

260. Are the first-borns required to listen to the *siyum*?

Ideally, they should listen to the conclusion of the volume studied. If they listened but did not understand, or if they missed the conclusion, they may nevertheless partake of the refreshments.

261. Must one eat a minimum quantity of the refreshments?

If possible, one should eat enough to make an after-*b'racha*.

262. What if there are not enough refreshments for all the first-borns?

If he heard the *siyum* he may break his fast at home, although ideally he should try to eat some of the refreshments provided at the *siyum*.

263. On completion of which volumes may one make a *siyum*?

A *siyum* may be made on completion of any one of the following:
- A tractate of Talmud *Bavli* or Talmud *Yerushalmi*.
- One of the six orders of the Mishnah.
- One of the books of the prophets studied in depth.
- One of the four volumes of the *Shulchan Aruch*.

264. May one deliberately hurry or delay the completion of a volume in order to make a *siyum* on *erev* Pesach?

Yes.

265. May a mourner participate in a *siyum*?

Yes. However, if he is in the week of *shiva* he may not go to shul, but he should arrange for someone to come to his house to make a *siyum*.

266. May first-borns participate in a *siyum* made by a boy below bar mitzvah?

Yes, as long as the boy studied the volume seriously and understood it to the best of his ability.

267. What if a first-born is unable to attend a *siyum*?

Ideally, he should try to fast all day, but if he has a headache or doesn't feel well he may break the fast. Similarly, if fasting will prevent him from properly fulfilling the mitzvos of the seder night, he need not fast. In either case, he should limit himself to just a small amount of food.

268. May one make or attend a *siyum* before *shacharis*?

Yes, but the refreshments must not be eaten until after *shacharis*.

Chapter Thirteen

Preparations for the Seder

The Wine and the Cup

269. Why do we drink four cups of wine?

This is a Rabbinic mitzvah that demonstrates our freedom, since wine is the drink of free men and nobility. The four cups correspond to the four terms of redemption used by Hashem when He promised to redeem the Jewish people from the bondage in Egypt (*Shemos* 6: 6-7).

270. Are red and white wines equally acceptable?

Red wine is preferred for two reasons:
- The red color indicates the wine's superiority.
- It is a reminder of the Jewish blood that was shed.

If the white wine is of better quality one may use it, but it is preferable to mix it with a little red wine to give it a red color. One should preferably pour the white wine into the red wine when mixing on Yom Tov.

271. May one use carbonated (sparkling) wine?

If it tastes like wine it is acceptable.

272. What if a person does not like wine?

A person who has difficulty drinking wine may use one that has a low alcohol content. Alternatively, he may mix wine and grape juice, taking care that there is still a taste of wine. One should be wary about diluting wine with water, since such a mixture may be invalid. Whoever exerts himself to drink the four cups of wine and eat the correct quantities of matzo even if he finds it difficult, will be spared from having to eat and drink bitter medicines. However, a person is not required to drink wine if it will make him ill.

273. May one use pure grape juice?

A person who cannot tolerate even weak wine, may use grape juice. Nevertheless, it is better to use a small cup of weak wine than a large cup of grape juice (see question 276).

274. May one use different wines for the four cups?

One should avoid switching wines during the seder, since a change from an inferior wine to a superior one may require a special *b'racha* (*hatov vehameitiv*). Therefore, a person should select the type of wine that he will enjoy drinking, and use it for all four cups. Alternatively, all the different wines should be placed on the table at the start of the seder. This mitigates the need for the special *b'racha*.

Chapter Thirteen - Preparations for the Seder

275. What if a person cannot tolerate either wine or grape juice?

He should use a drink that is considered to be the national beverage. A rav should be consulted to ascertain which drinks qualify for this purpose.

276. How large should the cup be?

According to the two main opinions, the cup must hold at least 86cc (approx. 3 fl. oz) or 150cc (approx. 5 fl. oz). Since the mitzva of drinking four cups of wine is rabbinic, one may be lenient to use the smaller quantity. When the seder is on Friday night, the first cup (Kiddush) is a Torah mitzvah and one is recommended to use the larger quantity. In any event, one should use a cup that holds slightly more than the minimum quantity, since wine often spills when holding the cup and when reclining.

277. How much of the cup should one drink?

Ideally, one should drink the entire cup, even if it contains more than the required amount. If this is not possible, it is sufficient to drink the majority of the cup. Therefore, it is better to use a small cup containing the minimum quantity that can be finished, than a large cup that cannot be finished.

278. How quickly should one drink the cup?

- Ideally, one should drink the cup without pausing.
- If this is not possible, one may stop once for a short pause during the drinking.
- If this too is not possible, one fulfills his obligation if he drinks the required quantity within four minutes.

279. May one use *shmittah* wine or grape juice?

It is preferable not to use this at the seder for two reasons:
- Wine usually spills during the seder and it is forbidden to cause *shmittah* wine to be wasted.
- The custom is not to drink the wine that is spilled at the ten plagues, and this would also be wasted (see question 392).

280. Who should pour the wine?

The leader of the seder should not pour his own cup, but another person should pour for him, since being served is a sign of freedom and nobility. Some have the custom that no one pours his own cup.

The Matzo

281. What is the difference between *shmura* matzo and regular matzo?

The Torah commands that matzo must be prepared under constant supervision to prevent it from becoming chometz. Matzo is called *shmura* if, in addition, it is made with the intention that it will be used to fulfill the mitzvah of eating matzo on the seder night (לשם מצות מצוה). Non-*shmura* matzo is not made with this additional intention.

282. Are both types of matzo acceptable for the seder?

No. Only *shmura* matzo is acceptable.

283. Is *shmura* machine matzo acceptable for the seder?

There is much controversy about this. According to some opinions, it is sufficient for the person who switches on the machine to have the correct intention. According to other opinions, this is not sufficient and machine matzos are invalid. One should follow the traditional custom to use handmade matzos, unless one has great difficulty in obtaining or eating such matzos.

284. Is there any advantage in using matzos made from hand-ground flour?

Shmura hand matzos are available in two types - those made from flour that is ground by hand and those made from flour ground by machine. Although some opinions disqualify the use of machinery for baking (see above), most opinions allow machinery to be used to grind the flour. The custom is to consider the machine-ground type just as acceptable, but it is praiseworthy to use matzos made from hand-ground flour.

285. Is there any advantage in eating only *shmura* matzos for the entire Pesach?

It is praiseworthy to do so, for two reasons:
- Some opinions require that the matzos for the entire Pesach be prepared with the same intention as those made for the seder (לשם מצות מצוה).
- *Shmura* matzo is usually supervised from the time that the grain is harvested. This is a higher degree of supervision than for regular matzo, which is supervised only from the time of grinding.

286. How much matzo must one eat to fulfill the mitzvah?

The quantity required for the mitzvah of eating matzo is a volume measure called a *kezayis*. The two widely accepted opinions regarding this measure are 30cc. and 50cc. When these figures are converted into weights, the measurements for a *kezayis* of matzo are approximately 15 grams and 25 grams. There is little difference between hand matzo and machine matzo.

287. Which opinion should one follow?

When performing a Torah obligation, one should preferably follow the stricter opinion (25 grams) and for a rabbinic obligation one may follow the lenient opinion (15 grams). In extenuating circumstances, one may be lenient to use smaller figures – 17 grams for a Torah obligation and 10 grams for a rabbinic obligation, e.g. for a sick or elderly person who finds it difficult to eat matzo.

288. At the seder, what is a Torah obligation and what is rabbinic?

There is a mitzvah to eat matzo three times during the seder:
- The first *kezayis* of *hamotzi*. This is a Torah obligation.
- For *korech* (the sandwich). This is a rabbinic obligation.
- For *afikoman*. This is rabbinic, but some opinions require a person to eat two *kezaysim*.

In *chutz la'aretz*, at the second seder, the first *kezayis* is also rabbinic.

Chapter Thirteen - Preparations for the Seder

289. How much matzo in total is a person required to eat?

The following chart should assist in making the calculations:

	First seder	Second seder	In case of difficulty or extenuating circumstances
Hamotzi	25g	15g	17g (10g at the 2nd seder)
Korech	15g	15g	10g
Afikoman	30g	30g	10g
Total	**70g**	**60g**	**37g (30g at the 2nd seder)**

It is advisable to eat slightly more than these quantities for two reasons:
• The figures are approximate and matzos vary in thickness.
• Some matzo is not eaten but falls to the floor or remains between the teeth, and this cannot be included in the quantity.

290. How much does an average matzo weigh?

• The weight of an average hand matzo is usually between 50 and 80 grams. To calculate the approximate weight of one's matzos one should divide the weight of the box by the number of matzos in the box.
• Machine matzos weigh approx. 30 grams.

291. Is it permitted to weigh the matzos on Yom Tov?

Although weighing is usually forbidden on Shabbos and Yom Tov, it is permitted for a mitzvah. Regular (spring) scales may be used, but not digital (battery or electric) scales. However, it is recommended that one weigh the matzos before Yom Tov in order to save time and frustration during the seder. It is also advisable to prepare in advance pieces of matzo weighing 15 grams and 25 grams in separate bags, that can be distributed during the seder without delay.

292. Should each person make an acquisition on the matzos that he intends to eat at the seder?

According to most opinions this is not necessary.

The Maror

293. Which foods may be used for *maror*?

Although the Sages list five types, the tradition has become unclear as to which species are intended. Only two are definitely known – lettuce and horseradish – and according to some opinions, a third is known to be endives. The widespread custom is to use lettuce or horseradish.

294. Which species is the most preferred?

Lettuce is the most preferred. However, there is a major problem that small insects are often found in lettuce and an experienced person must check the leaves. Today, insect-free lettuce is grown in greenhouses under special conditions, and this is obviously the best choice. (It should be rinsed well and checked minimally.) If a person can obtain only regular lettuce and he is afraid that it will not be checked meticulously, he should use the stems and/or hearts.

Alternatively, he should use horseradish, which is the second best species.

295. How can lettuce be used for *maror* if it is not bitter?

Although lettuce is usually sweet in taste, if it is left in the ground for a long time it becomes bitter. This resembles the way in which the Jewish people were treated in Egypt. When they first arrived they were settled in the best part of the land and were accorded the greatest honor and respect. Later, they were forced into slavery and their lives became bitter and miserable. According to most opinions, one may use lettuce even if it has no bitterness.

296. May the lettuce be left in water to keep it fresh?

Yes, but not for a continuous period of twenty-four hours. Lettuce will remain fresh for several days if kept in the fridge.

297. Should horseradish be eaten whole or grated?

It must not be eaten whole since this is dangerous. It should be grated on *erev* Pesach in order to release some of its sharpness and kept in a closed container until the seder. Grated horseradish that is mixed with beetroot juice (commonly called *chrain*) may not be used for *maror*.

298. What if one forgot to grate it on *erev Pesach*?

- If Pesach is a weekday, one may grate it in an unusual way. Either one should hold the grater upside-down while grating onto a plate, or one may hold the grater in the usual way but grate the horseradish onto a cloth or tabletop.
- If Pesach is on Shabbos, it is forbidden to grate even in an unusual way. The horseradish should be cut into small pieces with a knife just before the meal begins. The pieces should not be very small and certainly not chopped finely.

299. What if a person cannot obtain lettuce or horseradish?

He should use endives. However, a rav should be consulted since there are several varieties of this vegetable (e.g. escarole, chicory), and it is not clear which is the correct species. If this too is unavailable, he should use any bitter vegetable, but the special *b'racha* for the *maror* (*al achilas maror*) is not recited.

The Seder Plate

300. Which items should be placed on the seder plate?

There are seven items:
1. Three whole matzos.
2. A piece of roast meat or poultry.
3. A hard-boiled or roasted egg.
4. - 5. Two portions of *maror*.
6. *Charoses*.

Chapter Thirteen - Preparations for the Seder

7. *Karpas*.

In addition, salt water should be prepared, but the custom is not to place it on the seder plate.

301. What if a person has only two whole matzos (besides broken ones)?

He should use a broken one for the middle matzo, since this is anyway broken at *yachatz*.

302. How should the items be arranged?

Although there are several customs, the most widespread one is according to the *Arizal*. The arrangement is as follows:

Egg		Meat
	Maror	
Karpas		Charoses
	Maror	

303. Where should the matzos be placed?

- If one owns a purpose-built seder plate, the three matzos should be placed beneath these items.
- If not, the matzos should be placed on one plate and the remaining items on another plate nearby.

304. Must everyone have his own seder plate?

No, only the head of the household requires a seder plate.

305. Why are two portions of *maror* required?

The far portion is used when the *maror* is eaten the first time. The near portion is used when eating it the second time together with matzo (*korech*), and is usually referred to as *chazeres*. The same species of *maror* may be used for both portions.

306. Why do we use roast meat?

This is to remind us of the *korban* Pesach that was eaten roasted. This special piece is known as the *ze'roa* (arm) to recall the outstretched arm of Hashem that was displayed during the redemption from Egypt. It is not eaten at the seder (see question 438).

307. Which portion of meat should be used?

The shankbone, which is from the foreleg of the animal. If poultry is used, the custom is to use the wing or neck. If these are not available, any portion of roast meat or poultry may be used.

308. What if one forgot to roast it before Yom Tov?

It may be roasted on Yom Tov in the evening, but extra care must be taken to ensure that it is eaten during the day of Yom Tov (see question 438). If Yom Tov is on Shabbos, it may not be roasted in the evening.

309. Why do we use an egg?

This is to remind us of the *korban chagigah* (festival sacrifice). An egg is chosen for two reasons:

- The Aramaic word for an egg (*bai'yah*) also means to desire. This alludes to the fact that Hashem desired to redeem us.
- Eggs are eaten by mourners. This reminds us that we are unable to bring sacrifices due to the destruction of the Temple. (This is also alluded to in the calendar, which is arranged so that the first day of Pesach always occurs on the same day of the week as the following Tisha b'Av.)

310. Should the egg be roasted?

The main custom is to roast it, although a hard-boiled egg is also suitable. Some boil it and then roast it partially.

311. Should the egg be shelled before placing it on the seder plate?

The custom is to leave it in its shell.

312. When is the egg eaten?

The custom is to eat it during the seder (see question 435). Although it is forbidden to eat roast meat or poultry during the seder, it is permitted to eat roasted eggs.

313. What is *charoses*?

It is a mixture of finely chopped fruits, spices, and red wine. Traditionally, the fruits used are sour apples and nuts (particularly almonds) and the spices are cinnamon and ginger.

314. Why do we use *charoses*?

It is to remind us of the mortar used by the Jewish slaves in Egypt, and it should therefore be made to a thick consistency. Ideally, the spices should be fine strands to resemble the straw used to make the mortar. The sour apples remind us of the bitter slavery, and the wine reminds us of the Jewish blood that was spilled copiously during the years of hard labor.

315. What if one forgot to prepare it before Yom Tov?

It may be made in the evening in the normal manner. However, if Yom Tov is on Shabbos, it must be made with the following changes:

- The fruits should be cut into pieces with a knife. The pieces should not be very small and certainly not chopped finely.
- The wine should be put first into the mixing bowl, and the cut fruits added to it.
- The ingredients should be mixed with one's finger and not with a spoon or fork.

316. What is *karpas*?

It is a vegetable, preferably one that is eaten raw. The most commonly used are celery, sweet radish, cabbage, and parsley. Some use potato, although it is eaten only cooked. (Celery, cabbage, and parsley should be checked for insects.) Lettuce should not be used, since one may not use a vegetable that qualifies as *maror*.

Chapter Thirteen - Preparations for the Seder

Reclining

317. Why do we recline at the seder?

This is actually one of the four questions asked by the child (*ma nishtana*). The answer is that every person is required to feel on the night of Pesach as though he personally was a slave in Egypt and has just been granted his freedom. This mitzvah is one of the greatest challenges of the evening. While reciting the Haggadah and describing the extreme misery and sufferings of the Jewish people, a person must use his imagination to visualize himself in Egypt enduring the harsh slavery. When the discussion turns to the miraculous events leading to the Exodus, he must picture himself actually leaving Egypt to become a free man. When he eats and drinks on this night, he is required to recline, in order to demonstrate his newly gained freedom.

318. Should women recline?

The custom is that women do not recline. However, in order to demonstrate their feelings of freedom, they should sit in an armchair or a very comfortable chair.

319. Should children recline?

Boys aged nine or ten should be trained to recline. According to some opinions, they should be trained from the age of six.

320. Should a mourner recline?

Yes, but in a more modest fashion.

321. May a student recline in the presence of his Rebbe?

Since a student must respect and fear his Rebbe, he may not recline in his presence unless his Rebbe gives explicit permission. The custom is for the student to ask permission and for the Rebbe to grant it.

322. May a person recline in the presence of an outstanding Torah authority?

No one may recline in the presence of an outstanding Torah authority unless he receives explicit permission.

323. How should a person recline?

Ideally, he should sit in an armchair or on a chair with armrests, and lean to the left side. Preferably, a pillow or cushion should also be placed on the left side of the chair to support the body while reclining. This adds to the feeling of comfort and freedom.

324. What if he has only a regular chair?

He should recline on the table or on a second chair placed to his left. Alternatively, he may sit sideways and recline on the back of the chair. If possible, he should use a pillow or cushion to create a comfortable position. A person does not fulfill the mitzvah by leaning to the left in midair without supporting his body on anything, since this is not the way of free men.

325. May he lean on his left leg?

No, since he would appear to be worried rather than reclining in happiness. In extenuating circumstances, he may lean on another person's leg.

326. May a person recline on his back or to the right side?

No, since neither of these is the way of free men.

327. Why does reclining to the left demonstrate freedom more than to the right?

There are two reasons:
- The right hand must be free to hold the food.
- The food may ח"ו enter the wind-pipe when leaning to the right.

328. Should a left-handed person also recline on his left side?

Yes. Although this makes it difficult for him to eat, the danger of choking is the overriding consideration.

329. What if a person mistakenly reclined on his right side?

A right-handed person has not fulfilled his obligation, but a left-handed person has.

330. What if it is painful to recline on the left due to a wound etc.?

He is not required to recline.

331. When is one required to recline?

The minimum requirement is the following:
- When drinking the four cups of wine.
- When eating the first *kezayis* of matzo, the *korech*, and the *afikoman*.

It is praiseworthy to recline during the entire meal (see also question 439).

332. Should one recline while reciting the Haggadah?
No, one should sit upright with awe and respect.

General Points

333. May any type of food be served at the seder meal?
One must not eat poultry or meat that is prepared without any liquid. This includes roasted, barbecued, and broiled. The reason is that one should not mistakenly think that this is the actual *korban* Pesach (see also question 438).

334. May one eat pot roast?
- One may not eat poultry or meat that is roasted in a pot without any liquid. This applies even if it is first cooked with liquid.
- One may eat poultry or meat that is roasted in a pot with some liquid. This is permitted even if it is first roasted.

335. Why do some men wear a *kittel* at the seder?
- It is a garment of elevation reminding one of the angels. This enhances the feelings of freedom and royalty.
- It is garment of mourning, reminding one of the day of death. This has a subduing effect to prevent the feelings of royalty from leading to haughtiness.

336. Who should wear a *kittel*?

The main custom is that the person who leads the seder wears a *kittel*. In some communities all married men do so.

337. Should a mourner wear a *kittel*?

A mourner does not wear a *kittel* according to the main opinion.

338. Should a newly wed wear a *kittel*?

The main custom is that a newly wed (in his first year) does wear a *kittel*. (In any case, a newly wed usually celebrates the seder with his parents or parents-in-law and rarely leads the seder.)

339. How should the table be set for the seder?

The table should be covered with a white tablecloth. One should place on the table the most exquisite items of silver etc. that he possesses, in order to arouse feelings of freedom and royalty. Seating arrangements and preparations for reclining should be organized before Yom Tov, so that the seder can begin as soon as the men arrive home from shul after *ma'ariv*. Some have the custom to adorn the table with fragrant flowers. The word ריח (fragrance) has the same numerical value (218) as ליל פסח (the evening of Pesach).

340. What other preparations should be made before Yom Tov?

- Open all bottles of wine and grape juice, and boxes of matzo.
- Rinse all wine cups.
- Prepare a large and elegant cup for *Eliyahu Hanavi*.
- Prepare nuts and treats to give to the children before Kiddush and during the seder.
- People who bake their own matzos should verify that *challah* has been separated.
- In *chutz la'aretz*, *eiruv tavshilin* must be made when the first day of Pesach is a Thursday.

Chapter Fourteen
The Seder

Introduction

341. What does the word 'seder' signify?

The night of Pesach is indeed very different from all other nights of the year. It is steeped in holiness and abounds with mitzvos, both Torah and rabbinic, and is rich in customs and traditions. Every detail is of great significance and one should perform each step meticulously, knowing that no part of the procedure is trivial. The word 'seder' means order, indicating that the entire evening follows a set order, arranged by the Sages with holy inspiration and invested with hidden meanings and deep interpretations.

342. What are the main steps of the seder?

There are fifteen main steps, each of which has a special name. These names form a simple rhyme, thus becoming a memory aid to fulfilling the mitzvos of the evening in the correct order. They are:

    Kadesh, Urchatz, Karpas, Yachatz,
    Maggid, Rochtza, Motzi, Matzo,
    Maror, Korech, Shulchan Orech,
    Tzafun, Barech, Hallel, Nirtzah.

Many have the custom to announce each step with its name at the appropriate time.

343. What are the main mitzvos of the seder?

There are two Torah mitzvos – eating matzo and relating the story of the slavery and Exodus. There are three main rabbinic mitzvos – drinking four cups of wine, eating maror and reciting hallel.

344. What should be placed on the table before commencing the seder?

- The seder plate with all the necessary items (see question 300).
- A bowl of salt water.
- The wine and grape juice.
- A cup and a Haggadah for each participant.
- Elegant items of silver to decorate the table (see question 339)
- Flowers, to provide a pleasant fragrance (see question 339).

345. Should the father bless the children before commencing the seder?

Yes, this should be done as on Friday night. Indeed, the night of Pesach is particularly appropriate for blessing the children, since it was on this night that Yaakov *Avinu* received the blessings from his father Yitzchok *Avinu*.

346. Are women obligated in all the mitzvos of the seder?

Yes. Although these are time-bound mitzvos, women are obligated since they too experienced the terrible slavery and miraculous redemption. In addition, the

Jewish people were redeemed in the merit of the righteous women.

347. Are children obligated in all the mitzvos of the seder?

Children who have reached the age of *chinuch* (five or six) should try to fulfill all the mitzvos of the seder. Since their obligation is rabbinic, smaller quantities may be used for the mitzvos:

• The cup of grape juice (or wine) must contain the minimum quantity of 86cc (approx. 3 fl. oz.), but it is sufficient for them to drink a cheekful.

• For the three mitzvos of eating matzo (*hamotzi*, *korech*, *afikoman*) they can be given a small *kezayis* (10 grams), which should be eaten within nine minutes.

• For the two mitzvos of eating *maror* (*maror* and *korech*) they can be given a small *kezayis* (lettuce covering an area of 8" x 4"), which should be eaten within nine minutes.

• Boys who have reached the age of nine or ten should be taught to recline while drinking the wine and eating the matzo. According to some opinions, they should be taught from the age of six.

• Children should be encouraged to remain at the seder table at least until the end of the meal and if possible until after the fourth cup of wine. It is for this reason that the Sages instituted many unusual procedures during the seder, to arouse the interest of the children and hold their attention during the evening. The Torah requires a father to relate the story of the slavery and Exodus to his children, and the Haggadah emphasizes this by describing the four types of sons whom one may have to address. Some parents make the mistake of sending the children to bed after reciting the *ma nishtana* before they have heard the answers to their questions. It is advisable to see that the children sleep well on *erev* Pesach, in order that they will have the strength and enthusiasm to remain awake during the seder.

Kadesh – Recite Kiddush

348. Should the matzos be covered or uncovered during Kiddush?

They should be covered. The rule throughout the seder is that the matzos should be uncovered except when the wine is held. The reason is that matzo is a more important food than wine, and it should be covered when special attention is given to the wine.

349. Who recites Kiddush at the seder?

Some families have the custom that only the leader of the seder recites Kiddush and the other participants fulfill the mitzvah by listening. Some have the custom that everyone recites Kiddush together, including the women and children.

350. Should all the participants hold the wine during Kiddush?

Yes. All the participants should hold the wine during Kiddush, whether they are listening or reciting it.

351. Should women who have the custom to listen to Kiddush and have already recited the *shehecheyanu b'racha* when lighting candles say 'amen' to that *b'racha* during Kiddush?

Yes. The reason is that the *b'racha* recited when lighting candles refers only to the Yom Tov, whereas the *b'racha* recited during Kiddush refers to all the mitzvos of the seder.

352. Should women who have the custom to recite Kiddush and have already recited the *shehecheyanu b'racha* when lighting candles repeat that *b'racha* during Kiddush?

No, the *b'racha* must not be recited twice. If they prefer, they may delay reciting the *shehecheyanu b'racha* until during Kiddush.

353. What should one think about before reciting (or listening to) Kiddush?

- One should have in mind to fulfill two mitzvos:
  - The mitzvah of Kiddush.
  - The mitzvah of drinking the first of the four cups of wine.
- One should have in mind that the *shehecheyanu b'racha* applies to the Yom Tov and to all the mitzvos of the seder.
- Men should remember that they must recline when drinking the wine. They should also have in mind that they would like to drink another cup if they forget to recline (see question 356).

354. How much of the cup must be drunk?

Ideally, one should drink the entire cup, even if it contains more than the required amount. If this is not possible, it is sufficient to drink the majority of the cup.

355. How quickly must one drink the cup?
- Ideally, one should drink the cup without pausing.
- If this is not possible, one may stop once for a short pause during the drinking.
- If this too is not possible, one fulfills his obligation if he drinks the required quantity within four minutes.

356. What if a man forgets to recline?
- If he had in mind to drink another cup, he should do so immediately without speaking. If he accidentally spoke, he should not repeat any *brachos* before drinking again.
- If he did not have in mind to drink another cup, he should not drink again.

357. May one eat after Kiddush?

A healthy person should not eat any food before the meal except for the *karpas*. A sick or weak person may eat a small amount of food after Kiddush, except a vegetable. He should recite an after-*b'racha* before continuing with *urchatz*. Children may eat any amount of food, but not a vegetable.

358. May one drink after Kiddush?

One may have any drinks other than wine and grape juice between Kiddush and *urchatz*. Before Kiddush, one should have this in mind, and preferably place the drink on the table. The *b'racha shehakol* should not be recited over the drink. If he did not have this drink in mind, he should restrict himself to water, and recite the *b'racha shehakol*.

Urchatz — Wash the hands

359. Why are the hands washed now?
Although the meal is not yet served, the hands must be washed before eating the *karpas*. The reason is that one is required to wash hands without a *b'racha* before eating a food that has been rinsed or dipped in a liquid and is still moist. Some people are lenient about this throughout the year, relying on the opinions that say that this was necessary only in the time of the Temple. On the seder night everyone is particular to fulfill this mitzvah, since it is a time of extreme holiness (compare question 457). In addition, the children will notice something unusual and will be aroused to ask questions.

360. Who should wash hands at *urchatz?*
All the participants should wash their hands. In some families, only the leader of the seder washes his hands. Some have the custom that the leader of the seder has his hands washed by one of the children, in order to show freedom and royalty.

361. How should the hands be washed?
All the rules regarding washing for bread apply (e.g. removal of rings), except that a *b'racha* is not recited.

362. What if a person mistakenly recited the *b'racha*?

A person who recited the *b'racha* on the washing of the hands should eat a *kezayis* of *karpas*. Even though this quantity is eaten, an after-*b'racha* should not be recited.

363. Is it permitted to talk after washing the hands?

Care should be taken not to speak after the washing until the *karpas* is eaten, unless the talking is connected to the performance of the mitzvah.

Karpas – Eat the vegetable

364. Why do we eat *karpas*?

In order to stimulate the children to ask questions, since it is unusual to eat vegetables before the meal. The letters of the word *karpas* (כרפס) when reversed read ס' פרך, alluding to the 600,000 Jews (ס') who toiled in hard labor (פרך).

365. Why is the *karpas* dipped in salt water?

This is also one of the four questions asked by the child (*ma nishtana*). One answer is to stimulate the children to ask questions by doing something unusual. Another answer is that we dip in order to demonstrate our freedom, since it is the manner of royalty to eat their food in this way.

366. Who should dip the *karpas*?

There is no standard custom. Some find it convenient for the leader of the seder to dip several pieces of *karpas* into salt water before distributing them.

367. How much *karpas* should be distributed?

Each person should be given a piece less than a *kezayis*, i.e. less than 30cc (see also question 362).

368. Should one hold the *karpas* with a fork or with one's fingers?

The *karpas* should be held with one's fingers, since according to some opinions there would be no requirement to wash one's hands when eating with a fork. This is particularly important for those who use potato for *karpas*.

369. Who should recite the *b'racha* over the *karpas*?

The main custom is for each person to recite his own *b'racha*.

370. What should one think about before reciting the *b'racha* over the *karpas*?

Before reciting the *b'racha borei p'ri ha'adamah*, one should have in mind that this *b'racha* should include the *maror* that will be eaten later in the seder.

371. Should one recline when eating the *karpas*?

One is not obligated to recline but one may. The prevalent custom is to eat it without reclining.

372. What should be done with the remaining *karpas*?

It may be removed, but some have the custom to leave a piece of *karpas* on the seder plate until the meal. The salt water may be removed.

Yachatz – Break the middle matzo

373. Why is the middle matzo broken?

The Torah refers to matzo as 'the bread of the poor' (*Devarim* 16: 3), and a poor man usually eats pieces of bread, being unable to afford a whole loaf. The middle matzo is chosen since the special *b'racha* recited on the matzo (*al achilas matzo*) refers specifically to this matzo.

374. What should be done with the two pieces?

The smaller piece is returned to the seder plate and the larger one is wrapped up in a cloth and put aside to use as *afikoman*. The smaller piece should be at least a *kezayis*, and it is therefore advisable to select a large matzo for the middle matzo.

375. What if the larger piece will not provide the minimum quantity of matzo for *afikoman* for all of the participants?

Since this piece is usually not sufficient for all the participants, extra pieces of matzo should be prepared specifically for the *afikoman*.

376. Why do the children hide the *afikoman*?

It is a custom for the children to take the *afikoman* and hide it when the leader of the seder is not watching. This is to encourage the children to remain awake until the end of the meal when the *afikoman* is eaten.

Maggid – Relate the story of the Haggadah

377. What should one think about before beginning the narrative of the Haggadah?

Everyone should have in mind to fulfill the obligation to relate the story of the Exodus from Egypt. The mitzvah is fulfilled by relating three basic ideas:
- The wickedness of the Egyptians and the terrible sufferings that they afflicted upon the Jewish people during the long years of slavery.
- The miraculous plagues that Hashem brought upon the Egyptians, and the punishments meted out to them measure for measure.
- Thanks and praise to Hashem for the wonderful acts of kindness that He performed for the Jewish people, redeeming them from bondage and choosing them as His special nation.

All these aspects are elaborated upon during the recital of the Haggadah.

378. What if a person does not understand the text of the Haggadah?

The mitzvah is not fulfilled by mere recital of the Haggadah if the words are not understood. Those who are not familiar with Hebrew are strongly advised to spend time before Pesach studying the Haggadah, in order to turn the seder night into a deep and meaningful experience. It is a tragedy that so many people expend vast amounts of time and energy in preparing the house for Pesach, but are unable to find meaning and joy at the seder night. In any event, the leader of the seder must ensure that everyone understands at least the most essential sections of the narrative.

379. Which sections of the narrative are the most important?

- The ten plagues.
- From the section that begins 'Rabbi Gamliel used to say' until the second cup is drunk.

380. Must everyone recite the Haggadah or may one just listen?

Either method is acceptable as long as one understands what is being said. Most people follow the custom to recite the Haggadah if they are fluent in Hebrew.

381. Should anything be held when saying 'ha lachma anya'?

The leader of the seder should hold the broken middle matzo and show it to everyone. Some have the custom to hold all three matzos, while some have the custom to hold the entire seder plate with the matzos.

382. What is done after saying 'ha lachma anya'?

• The matzos should be removed from the table, or at least moved away from the leader of the seder. This is to arouse the interest of the children who should ask why the food has been removed before eating any of it. The father will then reply that we may not eat the meal until we relate the story of the Exodus.

• The second cup of wine is filled. This too should motivate the children to ask why we are having more wine before the meal.

• From this point until the second cup is drunk, it is forbidden to have any food or drink. Children may eat and drink freely.

383. Who should say *ma nishtana*?

The custom is for the youngest child capable of asking the questions to do so. If the child is hesitant, his father may assist him. If there are no children present, his wife or any of the participants should ask the four questions.

384. Should everyone repeat *ma nishtana* before continuing the Haggadah?

This is unnecessary, but some have the custom to do so.

385. What is done after saying *ma nishtana*?

The matzos should be returned to their place in front of the leader of the seder and left uncovered during the narrative (see question 348). The story of the slavery and Exodus is now related in detail.

386. How much time should be spent on narrating the story of the Exodus?

For most people it is sufficient to recite the standard text of the Haggadah pausing occasionally to elaborate on the essential sections. Analyses of the text are out of place at this stage, and a person should quote Midrashim and commentaries that describe the slavery and the miracles. It is important to explain the story to the participants according to the level of their understanding. In particular, one should try to hold the attention of the children during the narrative by describing the story as vividly as possible. One should keep an eye on the time, since every effort must be made to eat the *afikoman* before *halachic* midnight. As a rough guide, one should complete the narrative of the Haggadah and drink the second cup of wine approximately two hours before *halachic* midnight. If there is time to spare, one may expound on the story during the meal.

387. Does a convert recite the entire narrative?

Although some parts of the story do not seem to apply to a convert (e.g. we were slaves etc.), he should say the entire narrative. The reason is that his Jewish soul was enslaved in Egypt.

388. Should one recline during the narrative?

No, one should sit upright with awe and respect.

389. When does one spill out drops of wine?

- When saying the words דם, ואש, ותמרות עשן.
- When enumerating the ten plagues.
- When saying the three acronyms דצ"ך, עד"ש and באח"ב.

Thus a total of sixteen drops are spilled.

390. How should the wine be spilled?

Using the index finger. Some have a custom to use the little finger and some use the ring finger. If a person is too sensitive to use his finger, he should spill out the drops by tilting the cup.

391. What should one think about when spilling the wine?

That Hashem should protect us from such terrible plagues and bring them upon our enemies.

392. What should be done with the spilled wine?

It should be thrown away, since an impure spirit rests on it. For this reason, one should not use *shmitta* wine (see question 279).

393. Should the cups be refilled?

If necessary they should be refilled before saying 'Rabbi Gamliel etc.'

394. Should anything be held when saying 'This matzo etc.'?

Yes, the leader of the seder should hold up the broken middle matzo.

395. Should anything be held when saying 'This *maror* etc.'?

Yes, the leader of the seder should hold up the *maror*.

396. Should anything be held when saying 'The *korban* Pesach etc.'?

No. The shankbone is not held, since this would appear as if he is dedicating it as the *korban* Pesach. However, the custom is to look at the shankbone.

397. What should one think about when saying the paragraph 'In every generation etc'?

He should try to visualize himself in Egypt enduring harsh slavery, and then being redeemed miraculously by Hashem (see question 317).

398. When should the wine be held?

If possible, the wine should be held from the start of the paragraph 'Therefore we are obligated to thank etc.' until the wine is drunk. The matzos should be covered during this time. If it will be difficult to hold the wine for this length of time, one should hold the wine from the start of hallel. If this is also difficult, it is sufficient to hold the wine from the start of the *b'racha* '*asher ga'alanu'*.

399. What should one think before drinking the wine?

- To fulfill the mitzvah of drinking the second of the four cups of wine.
- If he intends to drink wine or grape juice during the meal, he should have in mind to include it with the *b'racha* recited on this second cup (see question 440).
- Men should remember that they must recline when drinking the wine.

400. What if a man forgot to recline?

He should immediately drink another cup without a *b'racha*.

Rochtza – Wash the hands

401. Why are the hands washed again now?

Although the hands were washed at the beginning of the seder (*urchatz*), they are now washed again before eating the matzo. The *b'racha al netilas yadayim* is recited. If a person is sure that his hands have not become *tamei* since the first washing, he should deliberately make his hands *tamei* before washing now. This can be done by touching one's shoes or scratching one's scalp.

402. What should be done before washing the hands?

- The leader of the seder should announce that one may not speak after washing the hands until after *korech*, unless it concerns the mitzvos.
- He should inform everyone about the next few steps of the seder, and tell them the relevant laws.
- Each person should be given a piece of matzo weighing at least 25 grams in preparation for the mitzvah of eating matzo (see question 287). Children may be given 10 grams each.
- The steps *rochtza*, *motzi*, and *matzo* should be announced.
- Some have the custom to ask one of the children to wash the hands of the father, in order to demonstrate freedom and royalty.

Motzi, Matzo – Two brachos are recited on the matzo

403. What should one think about before the *brachos* are recited?

- The leader of the seder should have in mind to include everyone else with his *brachos*.
- Everyone else should have in mind to fulfill his obligation by listening to the *brachos*.
- To fulfill the Torah mitzvah to eat matzo on the first night of Pesach.

- The *brachos* should also apply to the *korech* and *afikoman*.
- The men should remember to recline while eating the matzo.

404. Should the matzos be covered with a cloth?

Yes, they should be covered while the *b'racha* of *hamotzi* is recited.

405. Why are two *brachos* recited over the matzos?

The first *b'racha* is the regular *b'racha* of *hamotzi* recited over bread or matzo. The second *b'racha* – *al achilas matzo* – is recited for the mitzvah of eating matzo on the night of Pesach.

406. Which matzos are held?

All three matzos should be held for the first *b'racha*, after which the lowest matzo is released. The remaining two matzos are held for the second *b'racha*.

407. How should the matzos be broken?

Ideally, the two matzos should be broken simultaneously.

408. How should the matzos be distributed?

- The leader of the seder should take for himself 15 grams from the top matzo and 15 grams from the middle one. Both pieces should be eaten together.
- Everyone else should be given a small piece from the top matzo in addition to the prepared piece of 25

grams that was distributed before washing (see question 402). Both pieces should be eaten together.

409. Should the matzo be dipped in salt?
The main custom is not to dip it in salt.

410. How quickly should the matzo be eaten?
As quickly as possible, but in no more than two minutes. If this is difficult, it may be eaten within four minutes. This is measured from the time that one begins to swallow the matzo. One should nevertheless not eat in a state of frenzy or with voracity, but rather with dignity and joy as one fulfills the commandment of Hashem.

411. What if one's mouth is too dry to swallow the matzo?
One may drink a little water with it to facilitate swallowing.

412. What if a man forgot to recline while eating the matzo?
He must eat another *kezayis* while reclining. No *b'racha* is recited, but care should be taken not to speak before eating this matzo.

413. What if one ate the matzo without intention to fulfill the mitzvah?
One should eat another *kezayis* with the correct intention. No *b'racha* is recited. In *chutz la'aretz* on the second night, one is not required to eat another *kezayis*.

Maror – Eat the bitter herbs

414. How much *maror* should be eaten?

- If lettuce is used, one should eat a quantity that covers an area of 8" by 6" (20cm x 15cm).
- If grated horseradish is used, one should eat 27cc if possible. If this is difficult, it is sufficient to eat 17cc (approx. one heaped tablespoon).

415. May one combine lettuce and horseradish to make the required amount?

Since both are suitable species, one may combine them. Some have the custom to do this in order to feel some bitter taste, since the lettuce is not usually bitter.

416. How quickly should the *maror* be eaten?

As quickly as possible, but in no more than four minutes. This is measured from the time that one begins to swallow.

417. Why is the *maror* dipped in *charoses*?

Certain species of *maror* contain a dangerously bitter juice, and in order to neutralize this the *maror* is dipped into sweet *charoses*. In addition, the *charoses* is a reminder of the mortar used by the Jewish slaves.

418. Is thick *charoses* suitable for dipping?

Although the *charoses* is initially made thick to resemble mortar, it should be diluted considerably at this stage by adding more wine, making it suitable for dipping. The wine is also a reminder of the Jewish blood that was spilled copiously during the years of hard labor.

419. Should the entire portion of *maror* be dipped in *charoses*?
No, it is sufficient to dip some of it.

420. Who should recite the *b'racha* for the *maror*?
The custom is for each person to recite his own *b'racha*.

421. What should one think about before reciting the *b'racha* of *al achilas maror*?
- The *b'racha* should also apply to the *korech*.
- To fulfill the rabbinic mitzvah of eating *maror*.

422. What if one ate the *maror* without the intention to fulfill the mitzvah?
He should preferably eat another *kezayis*.

423. Should one recline while eating *maror*?
One does not recline, since the *maror* is a reminder of slavery and not of freedom.

424. What if a person is choking ח"ו over the horseradish?
He should immediately drink some hot water. This is a proven remedy.

Korech — Eat the sandwich of matzo and maror

425. Why do we eat matzo and *maror* together?

Although the vast majority of Sages said that matzo and *maror* should be eaten separately, it was the opinion of Hillel that they should be eaten together. On the seder night, we wish to fulfill both opinions and therefore we eat them first separately and then together.

426. Which matzo should be used?

The bottom matzo. Since this is usually not sufficient for everyone, the leader of the seder should distribute to each person a small piece from this matzo and supplement it with other matzo to make the required quantity.

427. How much matzo should be used for *korech*?

Each person should have 15 grams.

428. How much *maror* should be used for *korech*?

The same as for *maror* (see question 414).

429. Should the *maror* be dipped in *charoses*?

There are different customs, but the main custom is to dip it.

430. Should the *maror* be placed on the matzo or between two pieces of matzo?

The custom is to place the *maror* between two pieces of matzo.

431. Is a *b'racha* recited over the *korech*?

No, but a paragraph is said beginning with the words זכר למקדש כהלל. Although some opinions prefer the recital of this paragraph after eating the *korech*, the widespread custom is to recite it before eating the *korech*.

432. How quickly should the *korech* be eaten?

As quickly as possible, but in no more than four minutes. This is measured from the time one begins to swallow.

433. Should a man recline when eating the *korech*?

Yes.

434. What if he forgot to recline?

He does not need to eat another *korech*.

Shulchan Orech – Eat the Yom Tov meal

435. What should be served first?

The egg from the seder plate is distributed, dipped in salt water by some. Others do not eat this egg. Some have the custom to serve additional eggs.

436. Why are eggs eaten at the meal?
See question 309.

437. Should fish be served?
Some have a custom to eat fish, as a reminder that Hashem miraculously provided the Jewish women with fish, when they drew water for their exhausted husbands in Egypt.

438. Are there any restrictions relating to the meal?

- Roast meat or poultry should not be served (see question 333). The shankbone should also not be eaten.
- One should not eat excessively. Overeating may cause drowsiness and one will not be able to conclude the seder successfully. One must also remain with some appetite for the *afikoman* at the end of the meal.
- One must leave sufficient time after the meal to eat the *afikoman* before *halachic* midnight.
- If a dessert is served, one should avoid a fruit whose *b'racha* is *borei p'ri ha'adamah* since this raises a doubt whether the *b'racha* over the *karpas* includes such a dessert.

439. Should a man recline during the meal?
It is praiseworthy to do so, but not a requirement. Most men do not, since today we are not accustomed to recline, and it is difficult to eat comfortably and joyously in such a position.

440. Should one drink wine during the meal?

According to some opinions, it is a mitzvah to drink some wine during the meal in honor of Yom Tov.

441. Does the *charoses* require a *b'racha* if eaten during the meal?

- If the *charoses* is eaten together with matzo or other food, a *b'racha* is not required.
- If it is eaten on its own, a *b'racha* is required. If the fruit is recognizable the *b'racha* is *borei pri ha'eitz*, but if the fruit is not recognizable, the *b'racha* is *shehakol*.

Tzafun – Eat the afikoman

442. What does '*afikoman*' mean?

It means dessert. The last item of food eaten at the seder meal is a piece of matzo called the *afikoman*. The word '*tzafun*' means hidden, since the matzo is put away at the beginning of the seder, and reserved for *afikoman*.

443. Why is *afikoman* eaten?

In the days of the Temple, the last item of food eaten at the seder meal was the *korban* Pesach. Today, matzo is eaten instead, as a reminder of the *korban* Pesach.

444. Which matzo is eaten?

The piece of the broken middle matzo that was put aside at the beginning of the seder. Since this is usually not sufficient for everyone, the leader of the seder should distribute to each person a small piece from this matzo and supplement it with other matzo to make the required quantity.

445. How much matzo should be eaten?

If possible, each person should eat two *kezaysim* (30 grams). If this is difficult, he may eat one *kezayis* (15 grams).

446. Why are two *kezaysim* required?

In the days of the Temple, the *korban* Pesach was eaten together with matzo. Therefore, we eat one *kezayis* of matzo to remind us of the *korban* Pesach and another *kezayis* to remind us of the matzo that was eaten together with the *korban* Pesach.

447. Is a *b'racha* recited over the *afikoman*?

No, but one should have in mind to fulfill the mitzvah of eating the *afikoman*. Before eating the *afikoman*, some have a custom to recite a description of how the *korban* Pesach was prepared and eaten.

448. Should a man recline when eating the *afikoman*?

Yes.

449. What if he forgot to recline?

- If he has not yet washed his hands for *mayim acharonim*, he should eat another *afikoman* if this is not too difficult.
- If he has already washed hands for *mayim acharonim*, he should not eat another *afikoman*.

450. What is the latest time for eating *afikoman*?

Effort should be made to eat the *afikoman* before *halachic* midnight. Nevertheless, if this time passed, the *afikoman* should still be eaten.

451. What if the *afikoman* cannot be found?

Other *shmura* matzo should be eaten instead.

452. What if one forgot to eat the *afikoman*?

- If he has not yet *bensched*, he should eat the *afikoman* immediately. This is even if he has already washed *mayim acharonim*.
- If he has *bensched* but not yet drunk the third cup of wine, he should wash hands without a *b'racha*, recite *hamotzi*, eat the *afikoman* and *bensch* again.
- If he has already drunk the third cup of wine, he should proceed as in the previous case, except that he should *bensch* without a cup of wine. This should be done even if he has already drunk the fourth cup of wine.

453. May one eat anything else after the *afikoman*?

No, the *afikoman* must be the last food eaten at the seder, so that the taste remains in the mouth for the rest of the evening.

454. What if a person ate something after the *afikoman*?

He must eat another *afikoman* if possible.

455. May one drink anything after the *afikoman*?

Aside from the last two cups of wine one may drink water. Indeed, it is recommended to drink water after the *afikoman* if one is thirsty, since a person should not *bensch* while he is thirsty. One should preferably refrain from any other drinks, but in a case of great need one may drink tea, seltzer or mildly flavored soda. Coffee should not be drunk.

Barech – Bensch

456. When is the third cup of wine poured?

Before *bensch*ing. If necessary, the cups should first be rinsed.

457. Should one wash hands for *mayim acharonim*?

Even if a person is lenient about this during the year, he should be particular to wash hands for *mayim acharonim* at the seder, since it is a night of extreme holiness (compare question 359).

458. Who should lead the *bensching*?

If there are three men present, the custom is for the head of the household to lead the *zimun*. If there is an important visitor, he may be given this honor.

459. What should one think before *bensching*?

- To fulfill the Torah mitzvah of *bensching*.

- To fulfill the rabbinic mitzvah of drinking the third of the four cups of wine.

460. Should everyone hold the wine during *bensching*?

According to some opinions, everyone should hold the wine. According to other opinions, this is necessary only when there is no *zimun*.

461. When may the wine be put down?

Ideally, the wine should be held throughout the entire *bensching* until it is drunk. If this is difficult, it may be put down after '*al yechasreinu*', and picked up again before reciting the *b'racha* over the wine.

462. Should a man recline when drinking the wine?

Yes.

463. What if he forgot to recline?

He should not drink again.

464. What if a person forgot to say *ya'aleh ve'yavo* (or *retzei* on Shabbos)?

If he began the fourth *b'racha*, he must repeat *bensching*. If he realized after drinking the wine, he should repeat *bensching* with another cup of wine. However, the wine should not be drunk after *bensching*, but should be used for the fourth cup.

465. What is done after drinking the third cup?

- The cups are refilled with wine.
- An extra cup is filled, known as the cup of *Eliyahu Hanavi*. (Some have the custom to fill this cup before *bensching*.)
- The door is opened and the paragraph שפוך חמתך is recited. (Some have the custom to fill the fourth cup after this paragraph.)

466. Who should fill the cup of *Eliyahu Hanavi*?

The custom is for the leader of the seder to fill it. It should be a large and especially beautiful cup.

467. What is the meaning of this cup?

- It is a symbol of faith, that just as Hashem redeemed the Jewish people from the slavery in Egypt, so too will He send *Eliyahu Hanavi* to announce the final redemption from exile.
- It represents the fifth cup of wine corresponding to the fifth expression of redemption – "I will bring you to the promised land" (*Shemos* 6: 8 - compare question 269). Since there is a dispute whether this cup should be drunk, it is left until *Eliyahu Hanavi* can give us the final ruling.

468. What should be done with the wine from the cup of *Eliyahu Hanavi*?

Many have the custom to leave it covered on the table overnight and use it for Kiddush on Yom Tov morning. Others pour it back into the bottle.

469. Why is the door opened for שפוך חמתך?

In order to remember that Hashem protects the Jewish people on this night. In the merit of our faith in Hashem, we hope to be worthy to witness the coming of *Moshiach*, and the punishment of the nations who deny the existence of Hashem.

470. Is שפוך חמתך recited sitting or standing?

The custom is to recite it while standing.

Hallel – Recite the hallel

471. What should one think before reciting hallel?

To fulfill the mitzvah of reciting hallel.

472. Are women and children obligated to recite hallel?

Women are obligated to remain at the seder for hallel and the fourth cup of wine. Children (aged five or six) should be encouraged to do so if possible (see question 347).

473. Should one leave matzo on the table during hallel?

Some have the custom to do so.

474. Should one hold the cup of wine during hallel?

If possible, it is preferable for everyone to hold the cup during hallel until the wine is drunk. When reaching the verse 'I shall raise the cup of salvation', the cup should be raised slightly.

475. Should one recline during hallel?
No. One should sit upright with awe and respect (see also question 332).

476. Should any verses be recited responsively?
If there are at least three people present, including one's wife and children, the verses of הודו and אנא should be said responsively, as is done in shul. The leader of the seder should recite these verses and the others should respond.

477. What is the correct order for the different sections of the hallel?
The regular hallel is followed by twenty-six lines of כי לעולם חסדו and then by נשמת. There are different customs about when to say the paragraph יהללוך. The main Ashkenaz custom is to recite it in its usual place after the regular hallel, but without the concluding *b'racha*. The paragraph ישתבח is concluded with the regular conclusion of hallel, i.e. מלך מהולל בתשבחות. Some have the custom to conclude ישתבח in the same way that it is said during *shacharis*.

478. What if one mistakenly concluded יהללוך with its *b'racha*?
He should continue as usual, but the paragraph of ישתבח should not be concluded with a *b'racha* (i.e. stop before the word ברוך).

479. What should one think before drinking the fourth cup?

To fulfill the mitzvah of drinking the last of the four cups. Effort should be made to drink a *reviyis* in order to recite the after-*b'racha*.

480. Should a man recline when drinking the fourth cup?

Yes.

481. What if he forgot to recline?

He should not drink again.

482. Should everyone recite the after-*b'racha al hagefen*?

This *b'racha* is recited only if one drinks a *reviyis*. When reciting the *b'racha*, one should have in mind that it also applies to all the other three cups of wine.

483. What if a person is unable to drink a *reviyis*?

- If he drank a *reviyis* for the third cup of wine, he should recite the *b'racha al hagefen*.
- If he did not drink a *reviyis* for either the third or fourth cup, he should listen to someone else who is reciting the *b'racha* and have in mind to be included.

484. What if one forgot to include חג המצות in *al hagefen* (or רצה on Shabbos)?

The *b'racha* should not be repeated.

485. Is there a time limit for the fourth cup?

According to some opinions, one should try to drink the fourth cup before *halachic* midnight.

Nirtzah – The Seder is accepted

486. Is one obligated to say the final part of the Haggadah?

After the paragraph חסל סידור פסח, the final part of the Haggadah comprises songs of praise to Hashem. Since these songs were added later, a person who is completely exhausted is not obligated to say them.

487. What is the meaning of the song '*chad gadya*'?

This song should not be understood literally. It is explained by some of the greatest commentaries as an allegorical story imbued with hidden meanings and deep secrets. The Vilna *Gaon* interprets the song to be a detailed account of the history of the Jewish people from the days of Yaakov *Avinu* until the time of *Moshiach*.

488. Why do some people recite *Shir Hashirim* after the seder?

According to the Midrash, *Shir Hashirim* is an allegorical song describing the mutual devotion between Hashem and the Jewish people. Many of the verses refer to the miraculous Exodus from Egypt.

489. May one retire to bed immediately after the seder?

There is a mitzvah to remain awake as long as possible to study the laws of Pesach and to continue relating the miracles of the Exodus. If a person is overcome by sleep he is exempt. Similarly, if he will not be able to *daven shacharis* properly without a good night's sleep, he may retire to bed.

490. Should one recite the entire bedtime *shema*?

The custom is to recite only the first paragraph of *shema* and the *b'racha hamapil*. The reason is that the remaining verses are usually said as a protection from danger. On the seder night, this is unnecessary, since it is a night of Divine protection.

In the merit of our fulfillment of the mitzvos of the seder, may Hashem watch over and protect the entire Jewish nation, and speedily bring *Moshiach* and the final redemption.

Second seder in Chutz La'aretz

491. Are there any differences at the second seder in *chutz la'aretz*?

• The seder table must not be arranged until nightfall. If it is *motzai* Shabbos, the women should say *boruch hamavdil bein kodesh lekodesh* before beginning any work.

• When reciting the Haggadah and when eating the matzo, one should have in mind to fulfill a rabbinic mitzvah.

• For the first *kezayis* of matzo one may be lenient to eat 15 grams (see question 289). Nevertheless, the leader of the seder should eat 15 grams from the top matzo and 15 grams from the middle matzo. A sick or elderly person may be lenient to eat 10 grams if necessary (see question 287).

• Some have the custom not to hurry to eat the *afikoman* before *halachic* midnight.

• One may have any non-intoxicating drinks after the *afikoman*.

• One may retire to bed immediately after the seder.

492. Should a visitor from *chutz la'aretz* conduct a second seder in *Eretz Yisroel*?

Yes. The seder should be conducted exactly the same way as in *chutz la'aretz*.

493. Should a visitor from *Eretz Yisroel* join the second seder in *chutz la'aretz*?

- If he is living alone or with close family, he is not required to participate in the second seder.
- If he is living with close family but there are other visitors present, or he is living with other people, he is required to participate in the second seder.

494. How should such a visitor participate in the second seder?

He should participate fully in the entire seder, except that he should not recite the following *brachos*:

- Kiddush (indeed he must recite *havdalah* in private before the seder begins).
- *Borei p'ri hagafen* on the second and fourth cups of wine.
- *Asher ga'alanu* on the second cup of wine.
- *Al achilas matzo* and *al achilas maror*.
- The *b'racha* at the conclusion of hallel (i.e. *yishtabach*).

Instead, he should ask one of the participants to include him with these *brachos*. According to some opinions, he should recite the *b'racha al hagefen* after the first cup and recite *borei p'ri hagafen* on the second cup.

Chapter Fifteen
When Pesach falls on Sunday

When the first day of Pesach falls on Sunday, there are many changes to the usual sequence of events leading up to Pesach. This chapter deals with the most basic rules. In order to understand thoroughly the many complex details, one is strongly recommended to attend *shiurim* or seek expert advice.

495. When is the fast of the first-born?
This is on Thursday the twelfth of Nissan. A *siyum* is held as usual.

496. When is the search for chometz performed?
This is performed on Thursday night. The usual *b'racha* is recited and the nullification of chometz is said after the search.

497. When does the sale of chometz take place?
The sale of chometz is arranged by the rav during the fifth hour of Friday the thirteenth of Nissan.

498. When is the chometz burned?
All unwanted chometz should be burned before the end of the fifth hour on Friday morning. The second nullification is **not** said yet.

499. Until when may chometz be eaten on Friday?

Chometz may be eaten all day. This is an unusual feature of the schedule, that one may continue to eat chometz after the unwanted chometz has been burned. However, since the house is already clean for Pesach, it is recommended that one does not continue to eat chometz all day. No more chometz should be left for eating than is absolutely necessary for the meals on Friday night and Shabbos morning.

500. Are there any work restrictions on this Friday?

No. All forms of work including haircuts, laundering, and sewing are permitted (compare question 235).

501. Which preparations for the seder should be made on Friday?

All the preparations that are usually made on *erev* Pesach should be made on Friday. Those who use lettuce for *maror* must not leave it in water for a continuous period of twenty-four hours. Those who use horseradish may either grate it on Friday and keep it in a closed container, or grate it on *motzai* Shabbos in an unusual way (see question 298).

502. How are the Shabbos meals eaten?

The major challenge is how to eat bread in a house that is clean for Pesach. The simplest and most *halachically* acceptable solution is to eat kosher for Pesach food served on disposable plates. Small challos or pitta bread should be used for *lechem mishneh* in order to minimize the quantity of chometz used. After the meal, all unwanted chometz including crumbs must be destroyed by flushing it down the toilet. Disposable plates to which chometz may be stuck should be taken out of the house and left in a *hefker* place, e.g. public garbage containers (if there is an *eiruv*). In cases of need, any remaining chometz may be removed by a non-Jew.

503. May one eat egg matzo instead of bread?

Opinions differ about this and a rav should be consulted.

504. May one eat matzo for the Shabbos meals?

It is forbidden to eat matzo on this Shabbos, since it is *erev* Pesach (see question 243). According to the main custom, this includes Friday night. One may be lenient to give matzo to children who are below bar or bas mitzvah on Friday night, and to very young children on Shabbos morning (see question 244).

505. When is the Shabbos morning meal eaten?

On Shabbos morning, one should eat a meal with bread before the deadline time for eating chometz. It is praiseworthy to eat two meals with bread before the deadline with a break in-between. Preferably, the break should be half-an-hour, but if one is pressed for time even a shorter interval is sufficient. After the meal(s), the same procedure should be followed as after the

Friday night meal. Teeth should be cleaned with a dry toothbrush without toothpaste, or by eating a hard food such as a raw carrot.

506. When is the final nullification said?

This is said on Shabbos morning after all the remaining chometz has been removed. Special care must be taken to remember to say it before the end of the fifth hour. Since the chometz is not burned, there is a greater likelihood that one may forget to say the nullification.

507. May one sleep during the day to have strength for the seder?

This is permitted, but one should not say explicitly that this is why he is sleeping. When sending the children to bed one must be especially careful not to say that this is in order for them to stay up for the seder.

508. Is there a third meal in the afternoon?

One should daven *minchah* early, and then eat a substantial meal (*seudah shlishis*) without bread or matzo. After the start of the tenth *halachic* hour, foods containing matzo meal (e.g. *kneidlach*) may not be eaten, and other foods may be eaten in moderate amounts (see question 248).

509. When may one begin preparing the seder table?

No preparations may be made for the seder until *motzai* Shabbos. Women should say *baruch hamavdil bein kodesh lekodesh* before doing any work.

510. Are there any changes to the seder?

At the beginning of the seder, Kiddush and *havdalah* are combined (יקנה"ז). A *Havdalah* candle is not lit but the *b'racha* is recited on the Yom Tov lights. The *b'racha* over spices is not recited. If the family custom is to recite the Kiddush all together, the women should omit the third and fourth *b'rachos* (*borei me'orei ha'eish* and *hamavdil*) and listen to one of the men saying them. According to some opinions, women may recite these *brachos*. Regarding the *shehecheyanu b'racha*, see questions 351 and 352.

Chapter Sixteen

Chometz after Pesach

511. Is there any problem with chometz after Pesach?

It is forbidden to derive any benefit from chometz that was in the possession of a Jew during Pesach. Therefore, when buying chometz after Pesach from a Jewish store, one must be sure that the chometz was sold through a rav before Pesach.

512. May one buy immediately after Pesach chometz that was sold to a non-Jew?

Yes, this is perfectly acceptable. Some have a custom not to buy food that is definitely chometz (see question 167) until there is a fresh supply manufactured after Pesach. This is due to concern that the store purchased it after Pesach from a non-religious supplier who owned it during Pesach. Strictly speaking, one may buy chometz if there is a reasonable doubt whether it was in the possession of a Jew during Pesach

513. May one buy questionable chometz immediately?

Yes. There is no reason to be stringent regarding questionable chometz that was sold through a rav (see question 169). For example, one may buy flour that was sold, and chometz products that were made after

Pesach from such flour. There is no need to wait for freshly ground flour and products made therefrom.

514. What about buying *kitniyos* and medicines?

It is permitted to buy *kitniyos* and medicines immediately after Pesach from any store, even if the storekeeper did not sell the chometz before Pesach.

Chapter Seventeen

Chodosh

515. What is *chodosh*?

Chodosh literally means 'new'. This refers to grain that was planted after Pesach or shortly before Pesach but did not take root until after the second day of Pesach. The Torah forbids eating such 'new' grain and any products made from it, until after the second day of Pesach the following year. It is then called '*yoshon*', literally 'old', and may be eaten. Grain that took root before Pesach is permitted immediately after Pesach.

516. Does this apply to all grains?

No, it applies only to the following five grains: wheat, barley, spelt, rye, and oats. Other grains such as rice, corn, buckwheat, millet etc. are not included in this prohibition.

517. Does this apply to *chutz la'aretz*?

According to most opinions, *chodosh* applies to grains that are grown in *Eretz Yisroel* or in *chutz la'aretz*.

518. Does it apply to grain grown by gentiles?

According to most opinions, it applies also to grain grown by gentiles.

519. Why do many kashrus organizations permit *chodosh* to be eaten?

For many hundreds of years, people have been lenient about eating *chodosh*, relying on minority opinions that allow grain from *chutz la'aretz* or gentile grain. This was due to the difficulty in obtaining *yoshon* at certain times of the year and the fact that grain is an essential commodity that one cannot live without. Another factor was that one could not know whether a particular grain was *chodosh* or *yoshon* and in a case of doubt such as this, many opinions are lenient.

520. Should one be strict to avoid *chodosh*?

It is praiseworthy not to rely on the lenient opinions, and try to avoid eating *chodosh*. In recent years there has been increasing interest in this matter, and some kashrus organizations are certifying their products as *yoshon*.

521. How widespread is the problem of *chodosh*?

The problem is almost non-existent with foods manufactured in *Eretz Yisroel*, but it does exist with imported foods. This is because grain is planted in *Eretz Yisroel* at the beginning of winter and harvested only after Pesach, rendering it all *yoshon*. In *chutz la'aretz* the problem is greater. For example in America, spring wheat is often planted after Pesach and reaches the market at the end of the summer. This is *chodosh* until the following Pesach. Similarly, oats and barley in America are summer grains and are *chodosh* until Pesach. Rye in America is a winter crop and is *yoshon*.

522. What if a product contains a mixture of *chodosh* and *yoshon*?

This is a common situation. For example, rye bread in America is made from a minority of rye flour and a majority of spring wheat flour giving it *chodosh* problems. Similarly, many foods contain malt made from barley that may be *chodosh*. Malt is used for making beer and as a flavoring in cereals, cookies, candies, and vinegar. If the *chodosh* ingredient is the majority or can be tasted, then the product is considered *chodosh*. If it is the minority and cannot be tasted, according to some opinions the product is *yoshon* but others regard it as *chodosh*.

523. Which time of year is most problematic?

This varies from country to country, but generally the problematic time is from Succos until Pesach. There are no problems of *chodosh* during the months immediately following Pesach. After that time, a problem may exist since some new grains may become available towards the end of the summer.

Guide to Chometz items

Definite chometz - Must not be owned during Pesach but sold to a non-Jew and put out of sight (see questions 165 and 175). This includes:
Beer, biscuits, bissli, bran, brewers yeast (nutritional yeast), cake, cereals (that contain one of the five grains), cookies, crackers, dough, drinks from grains (chico), instant quaker oats, macaroni, malt, noodles, oatmeal, puffed wheat, semolina, snack bars (that contain one of the five grains), soup nuts, spaghetti, wafers, wheat germ, whisky, yeast extracts. [The five grains are wheat, barley, spelt, rye, and oats].

Items that are questionable whether they are chometz - should not be used but may be sold to a non-Jew and put out of sight. This includes:
Alcohol, alcoholic drinks (except beer and whisky), all canned foods, baked beans, baking powder, burgol (whole wheat), brown sugar, candies, chewing gum, chocolate spread, cocoa, coffee, custard powder, dextrose, dried fruit, drinking chocolate, falafel powder, flavorings, flour, fruit drinks, glucose, granola, grape sugar, instant puddings, pleasant tasting medicines, mustard, pearl barley, pickled meats, pickled vegetables, play-do, powdered soups, raw oats, regular matzo and matzo meal, salted nuts and seeds, sausages, soda, starch, spices, vegetarian meat, vinegar, vitamins.

***Kitniyos* products** - that are not supervised for Pesach should be put away and sold, since they may contain questionable chometz. This includes:
Bamba, cornflakes, corn flour, corn oil, dextrose, glucose, lecithin, mustard, peanut butter, peanut oil, popcorn, sorbitol, soy oil, starch, and tehina. Chocolate, margarine, mayonnaise, and salad dressing are usually made from *kitniyos* and must have a *hechsher* for Pesach.

Pure *kitniyos* - do not need to be sold or put out of sight. This includes:
Alfalfa, aniseed, beans, buckwheat, caraway, chickpeas, coriander, cumin, fennel, fenugreek, flax, lentils, maize, millet, mustard, peas, peanuts, poppy seeds, rice, sesame, soy, sunflower seeds, and tofu.

Not chometz at all - May be used on Pesach. Some have a custom not to use the *italicized* products unless they have a *hechsher*. This includes:
Acetone, air fresheners, eardrops, eye drops, hair spray, medicinal creams, nail polish, nose drops, talc, throat sprays, *bitter or tasteless medicines, cologne, cosmetics, deodorants, hair spray, hand cream, mouthwash, perfume, shampoo, soap*.

Glossary

Al hagefen - *B'racha* recited after drinking wine or grape juice.

Al netilas yadayim - *B'racha* recited over the mitzvah of washing the hands.

Arizal - Rabbi Yitzchak Luria (1534-1572), considered to be one of the greatest kabbalists.

Ashkenaz - German or Polish Jewry.

Av harachamim - Prayer in memory of Jewish martyrs.

Bamidbar - The book of Numbers.

Bedikas chometz - The search for chometz.

Bensch - To recite grace after meals.

Benschers - Book from which *bensching* is recited.

Blech - Metal sheet used to cover the stove on Shabbos.

Borei p'ri ha'adamah - *B'racha* recited over vegetables (lit. who creates the fruit of the ground).

Borei p'ri ha'eitz - *B'racha* recited over fruit (lit. who creates the fruit of the tree).

Borei p'ri hagafen - *B'racha* recited over wine and grape juice (lit. who creates the fruit of the vine).

B'racha (pl. *brachos*) - A blessing.

Bris - Circumcision.

Challah - Tithe taken from dough.

Chinuch - Education.

Chol hamoed - The intermediate days of the festival.

Chometz - Leaven, which may not be owned or eaten during Pesach.

Chosson and kallah - Newly married couple.

Chumash - Book containing the five books of Moses.

Chutz La'aretz - The Diaspora.

Daven - To pray.

Devarim - The book of Deuteronomy.

Eiruv - Enclosure of a public domain which transfers it into a private one in order to permit objects to be carried on *Shabbos*.

Eiruv Tavshilin - Foods prepared before Yom Tov to allow preparations to be made on Friday for Shabbos. This is required when Yom Tov is on the day(s) immediately preceding Shabbos.

Eliyahu Hanavi - Elijah the prophet.

Eretz Yisroel - The land of Israel.

Erev Pesach - The day before Pesach.

Erev Shabbos - The day before Shabbos.

Erev Yom Tov - The day before a festival.

Haftorah - Public reading from Prophets.

Halacha (pl. *halachos*) - Jewish law.

Halachic dawn - 72 *halachic* minutes before sunrise.

Halachic hour - 1/12 day, reckoned from sunrise to sunset (or dawn to nightfall).

Halachic midday - The midpoint between sunrise and sunset.

Hallel - Psalms of praise recited on festive days.

Hamotzi - The blessing recited over bread (lit. 'who takes bread out of the ground').

Hashem - G-d.

Havdalah - Prayer recited at the conclusion of Shabbos and festival to divide between a holy day and a weekday.

Hechsher - Rabbinical supervision.

Kabbalah - Jewish mysticism.

Kasher - To make a utensil kosher.

Kashrus - Matters concerning kosher items.

Kebeitza - A volume measure (approx. 60 cc).

Kel erech apayim - Prayer recited before the reading of the Torah.

Glossary

Kel malei rachamim - Memorial prayer.

Kezayis (pl. *kezaysim*) - A volume measure (approx. 30 cc).

Kiddush - Sanctification of Shabbos and festivals, usually recited over a cup of wine.

Kittel - White outer garment.

Kneidlach - Boiled matzo-meal balls.

Korban Pesach - Pesach Sacrifice.

Lamnatzeach - Psalm 20, recited towards the conclusion of *shacharis*.

Lechem Mishneh - Two complete loaves used on Shabbos and festivals as a commemoration to the double portion of Manna that fell on *erev* Shabbos.

Lulav - Four species that are taken on Succos.

Ma'ariv - The evening prayer.

Mayim acharonim - The water with which the hands are washed immediately prior to *bensching*.

Mezuzah (pl. *mezuzos*) - Parchment scroll on which parts of the Torah (including the *shema*) are written. The scroll is affixed to the doorway of every room.

Midrash - Commentary on the Bible.

Mikveh - Ritual immersion pool.

Mincha - The afternoon prayer.

Mincha gedolah - The earliest time when the *mincha* prayer may be recited.

Minyan - Quorum of men required for communal prayer.

Mishnah - The basis of the oral law.

Mitzvah (pl. Mitzvos) - A commandment.

Mizmor lesodah - Psalm 100, recited during *pesukei d'zimra* on weekdays.

Moshiach - The messiah.

Motzai Shabbos - The day after Shabbos.

Nesi'im - Leaders of the twelve tribes.

Orlah - Third year produce of fruit trees which is forbidden.

Pesukei d'zimra - Verses of praise recited at the beginning of *shacharis*.

Pidyon haben - Redemption of the firstborn.

Posek - *Halachic* authority.

Purim - One of the minor festivals.

Rav (pl. *Rabbonim*) - Rabbi.

Retzei - Paragraph added to *bensching* on Shabbos.

Reviyis - Liquid measure (86cc or approx. 3 fl. oz.).

Rosh Chodesh - The first day of the new month.

Sefer Torah (pl. *Sifrei Torah*) - Hand written scroll of the five books of Moses.

Sephard - Spanish, Portugese, or North African Jewry.

Seudah Shlishis - Third meal that is eaten on Shabbos.

Seudas Mitzvah - Meal eaten to celebrate a *mitzvah*, e.g. wedding, circumcision, redemption of the firstborn etc.

Shacharis - The morning service.

Shechina - The Divine presence.

Shehakol - *B'racha* recited over food.

Shehecheyanu - The blessing made to thank *Hashem* for bringing us to the time when we can benefit from a new item or perform a new *mitzvah*.

Shemoneh Esrei - Supplication that forms a central part of formal prayer. On a weekday this contains 19 blessings.

Shemos - The book of Exodus.

Shir Hashirim - The Song of Songs.

Shiur (pl. *shiurim*) - A lesson in the Torah.

Shiva - The week of mourning after the passing of a close relative.

Shloshim - The thirty-day period after the passing of a close relative.

Shmitta - The final year of the seven year agricultural cycle.

Shofar - Ram's horn blown at the New Year.

Shulchan Aruch - Code of Jewish law.

Siddur - Prayer book.

Siyum - Festive meal made at the conclusion of a tractate etc.

Succos - Feast of Tabernacles.

Tachanun - Prayer recited immediately following *Shemoneh Esrei*.

Talmid chochom - Torah scholar.

Tamei - Spiritually impure.

Tanach - The Bible.

Tisha B'Av - Ninth of Av, day of mourning and fasting.

Treif - Non-kosher food.

Tu bi'shvat - The 15th of Shevat, the new year for trees.

Tzaddik (pl. *Tzaddikim*) - Righteous individual.

Tzidkascha - Prayer recited during *mincha* on Shabbos.

Vilna Gaon - Rabbi *Eliahu* (1720-1797), Genius of Vilna and leader of Eastern European Jewry.

Yaakov Avinu - Jacob the Patriarch.

Ya'aleh ve'yavo - Additional prayer recited on Yom Tov and *Rosh chodesh*.

Yahrzeit - Hebrew date on which a person died.

Yishtabach - Concluding paragraph of *pesukei d'zimra*.

Yitzchak Avinu - Isaac the Patriarch

Yom Tov - A festival.

Zimun - Invitation to *bensch*, made in the presence of at least three men.

Index

Afikoman
  cannot be found......... 140
  drinking afterwards 141
  eating afterwards 140
  forgot to eat 140
  forgot to recline 139
  hidden by children...... 123
  latest time to eat........ 140
  origin 138
  quantity required........ 139
  rabbinic obligation........ 98
  reciting *b'racha* over ... 139
  recline........................ 139
  second seder 149
  two portions 139
  which matzo 138

After-*b'racha*
  after the fourth cup 146
  not recited after *karpas*120
  person who ate after Kiddush................... 118

B'racha
  al hagefen 146
  al netilas yadayim....... 129
  asher ga'alanu 129
  bedikas chometz30, 74, 75, 76, 78, 80
  hallel......................... 145
  hamapil..................... 148
  hatov vehameitiv.......... 94
  kashering utensils......... 48
  over *afikoman*............. 139
  over *charoses* 138
  over *karpas* 121
  over Kiddush.............. 117
  over *korech* 136
  over *maror* 102, 134
  over matzo 131
  repeating *shehecheyanu*117
  trees in blossom..... 18, 19
  urchatz (before *karpas*)119

Barech
  forgot *ya'aleh ve'yavoh*142
  washing *mayim acharonim* 141

Bedikas chometz
  before the fourteenth ... 80
  davening ma'ariv before 72
  distributing ten pieces of bread...................... 78
  eating before............... 73
  ideal time.................... 72
  intention before........... 75
  more than one property 76
  Pesach on Sunday.......151
  reciting *b'racha*.......74, 75
  sleeping before............ 74
  sold areas 77
  speaking during search. 76
  using flashlight 78
  visitors........................ 80
  what to look for........... 76
  where to look 77
  women's obligation 74
  working before 73
  yeshiva students.......... 81

Bensching
  forgot *ya'aleh ve'yavoh*142
  intention before 141
  washing *mayim acharonim* 141
  who should lead *zimun*141

Benshers
  cleaning 25

Blech
  kashering 35

Blender
  kashering 40

Blessing children
  before seder...............114

Bookcase
  cleaning 25

Books
  cleaning 25

Burners
  kashering 34

Index

Burning chometz
　Pesach on Sunday 151
　what should be burned . 82
　when 83
Carpet
　cleaning 28
Chad gadya
　significance................ 147
Chairs
　cleaning 27
Charity
　obligation to give before Pesach 17, 18
Charoses
　composition 105
　dipping *korech* into..... 135
　dipping *maror* into...... 133
　reciting *b'racha* over during meal 138
Chazeres
　on seder plate............ 104
Children
　blessing before seder.. 114
　eating after Kiddush ... 118
　eating matzo on *erev* Pesach 86, 153
　four cups.................... 115
　giving them treats 112
　hallel........................... 144
　hide *afikoman*............. 123
　kitniyos 63
　maror.......................... 115
　matzo 115
　obligation in mitzvos of the seder 115
　reclining 107
　resting before seder .. 115, 154
Chodosh
　definition.................... 158
　extent of problem....... 159
　in *chutz la'aretz*.......... 158
　which grains 158
Choking
　on horseradish 134

Chometz
　burning....................... 82
　buying after Pesach.....156
　limitations in eating 82, 152
　obligation to remove 24
　owned during Pesach ..156
Chometz after Pesach
　prohibition 156
Chutz la'aretz
　chodosh.....................158
　eiruv tavshilin.............112
　visitor from *Eretz Yisroel*150
Cleaning
　attitude towards 23
　benshers..................... 25
　books 25
　broom 30
　carpet......................... 28
　chairs 27
　clothes........................ 26
　couch 27
　crumbs 24
　dental apparatus.......... 29
　floor 28
　freezer........................ 39
　fridge.......................... 38
　high chair.................... 27
　house vacant during Pesach 30
　kitchen 32
　kitchen cabinets........... 42
　moving furniture.......... 24
　pots............................ 42
　rings (jewellery)........... 29
　table........................... 26
　toaster........................ 40
　toys............................ 25
Clothes
　cleaning 26
　laundering *erev* Pesach 85, 152
Cloves
　custom not to eat 51
Convert
　fast of the first-born..... 89
　maggid 127

Cosmetics
   using............................ 57
Couch
   cleaning 27
Crumbs
   cleaning for Pesach 24, 28, 32, 84
Cup of *Eliyahu Hanavi*
   significance................. 143
   when filled.................. 143
   who fills 143
Dental apparatus
   cleaning 29
Dip
   egg in salt water 136
   karpas in salt water 121
   maror in *charoses*133, 135
   matzo in salt............... 132
Dishwasher
   kashering 36
Dried fruits
   supervision 51
Egg matzo
   Pesach on Sunday 153
Eggs
   washing 52
Electric hot plate
   kashering 35
Electric stove
   kashering 35
***Erev* Pesach**
   cutting hair 85
   cutting nails 85
   davening mincha........... 87
   eating chometz 82
   eating *kitniyos* 87
   eating matzo................ 86
   eating matzo meal........ 87
   fast of the first-born *See* Fast of the first-born
   immersing in *mikveh* 88
   ironing clothes 86
   laundering clothes........ 85
   sewing 86
   working........................ 85

Fast of the first-born
   attending *siyum*............ 90
   attending *siyum* before *shacharis* 92
   child 90
   child born by caesarean 90
   convert 89
   eating at *siyum*............. 91
   mourner participating in *siyum* 91
   origin and significance.. 89
   Pesach on Sunday.......151
   when 89
   which first-borns.......... 89
First cup (Kiddush)
   eating after 118
   forgot to recline..........118
   intention before drinking117
Floor
   cleaning 28
Floor cleaner
   using 55
Flour
   buying products made from after Pesach 157
Flowers
   adorning seder table with 111
   selling dried arrangements 68
Forgot to recline
   afikoman.....................139
   first cup (Kiddush) 118
   fourth cup (after hallel)146
   korech 136
   matzo 132
   second cup (after *maggid*) 129
   third cup (*barech*).......142
Four cups
   carbonated wine 93
   children 115
   grape juice 94
   national beverage 95
   poured by another person96
   quantity required 95

Index

red wine 93
shmittah wine 96
size 95
Fourth cup (after hallel)
   cup filled 143
   forgot to recline 146
   intention before drinking 146
   recite an after-*b'racha* following 146
Freezer
   cleaning 39
   storing chometz in during Pesach 39
Fridge
   cleaning 38, 39
   cleaning underneath 24
   storing chometz in during Pesach 39
   storing *kitniyos* in during Pesach 63
Fruits
   peeling 52
Garlic
   custom not to eat 51
Gebroktz
   definition 64
   preferable than *kitniyos* 65
   reason behind 64
Grape juice
   using for four cups 94
Grates
   kashering 34
Haggadah
   reclining 110
Hallel
   children 144
   correct conclusion 145
   holding wine during 144
   intention before 144
   matzo left on table 144
   reciting responsively ... 145
   reclining during 145
   women's obligation 144
Herbs
   supervision 52

High chair
   cleaning 27
Horseradish
   combining with lettuce 133
   remedy if choking over 134
   using for *maror* ... 133, 152
Intention before
   bedikas chometz 75
   bensching 141
   drinking the first cup ... 117
   drinking the fourth cup 146
   drinking the second cup 129
   drinking the third cup .. 141
   eating *afikoman* 139
   eating *karpas* 121
   eating *maror* 134
   eating matzo 130
   reciting hallel 144
   reciting the Haggadah . 123
Karpas
   dipping in salt water 120
   holding with fingers 121
   intention before eating 121
   origin and significance . 120
   quantity eaten 121
   reclining 122
Kashering
   blech 35
   blender 40
   burners 34
   dishwasher 36
   electric hot plate 35
   electric stove 35
   grates 34
   kitchen counter 41
   microwave 35
   mixer 40
   new utensils 48
   oven 33
   pot cover 47
   pressure cooker 47
   self-cleaning oven 33
   Shabbos kettle 36
   sink 36, 37
   sink faucets 37
   sink spout 37

standard methods 45
stove tray 34
which materials............ 45
who should perform 45
Kiddush
eating after................ 118
forgot to recline 118
matzos covered.......... 116
who recites................ 116
women reciting
shehecheyanu........ 117
Kitchen
importance in cleaning.. 32
kashering *blech*............ 35
kashering blender......... 40
kashering burners 34
kashering counter 41
kashering dishwasher ... 36
kashering electric hot plate
.... 35
kashering electric stove. 35
kashering grates 34
kashering microwave.... 35
kashering mixer 40
kashering oven 33
kashering sink........ 36, 37
kashering sink faucets .. 37
kashering sink spout..... 37
Kitchen cabinets
cleaning 42
Kitchen counter
kashering 41
Kitniyos
buying after Pesach.... 157
children...................... 63
common examples 60
derivatives................... 61
erev Pesach 62
exceptional circumstances 61
preparing on Pesach stove
.... 62
reason not eaten.......... 60
selling 62
selling products............ 63
storing in fridge during
Pesach 63

Kittel
wearing 110
Korech
origin.........................135
quantity of *maror* required
.............................135
quantity of matzo required
.............................135
rabbinic obligation........ 98
reciting *b'racha*...........136
reclining.....................136
which matzo...............135
Leaning
at Seder .... See Reclining
Lettuce
combining with horseradish
.............................133
using for *maror*...........133
Lipstick
using 57
Ma nishtana
repeating 126
who should say...........125
Maggid
basic ideas 123
convert......................127
elaborating.................126
in English 124
listening.....................124
reclining.....................127
visualize in Egypt 128
Maror
combining lettuce and
horseradish 133
dipping in *charoses* 133
grating horseradish 102
intention before eating 134
quantity required 133
reciting *b'racha*...........134
remedy if choking over 134
two portions...............104
which species 100
Matzo
average weight............ 99
break into two 122
children 115

Index

cover before reciting *b'racha* 131
dipping in salt 132
distributing 131
forgot correct intention 132
forgot to recline 132
hand-ground flour 97
intention before eating 130
limitations in eating 16, 86, 153
made by machine 97
manner of eating 132
quantity required 98
shmura 96
special *b'racha* 131
Torah obligation 98
total requirement 99
weighing on Yom Tov ... 99
Medicinal creams
using 56
Medicine
buying after Pesach 157
taking 56
Microwave
kashering 35
Mikveh
immersing *erev* Pesach . 88
Mixer
kashering 40
Mourner
participating in *siyum* 91
reclining 107
wearing *kittel* 111
Nirtzah
significance 147
Nissan
b'racha recited over trees 18, 19, 20, 21
changes to prayer 16
fasting during 17
special significance 15
visiting cemetery 17
Nullification of chometz
Pesach on Sunday 154
reason said twice 84
when 79, 84, 85

which language 79
who 85
Opening door
significance 144
when 143
Oven
kashering 33
using before Pesach 33
Paperware
using 59
Perfume
using 57
Pesach on Sunday
basic laws 151
bedikas chometz 151
burning chometz 151
egg matzo 153
fast of the first-born 151
limitations in eating chometz 152
selling chometz 151
Pet food
using 58
Plasticware
using 59
Pots
scrubbing clean 42
selling during Pesach 68
storing during Pesach ... 42
Prayer
changes during Nissan .. 16
changes on *erev* Pesach 82
Pressure cooker
kashering 47
Quantity required
afikoman 139
four cups 95
karpas 121
korech 135
maror 133
matzo 98
Reclining
afikoman 139
children 107, 115
during meal 137
fourth cup 146

karpas 122
korech 136
left-handed person 109
maggid 127
maror 134
matzo 132
mourner 107
origin and significance 107, 145
third cup 142
when required 109
which direction 109
with a cushion 108
women's obligation..... 107
Rings
cleaning 29
Roasted meat
serving at seder .. 110, 137
Rochtza
origin 129
Second cup (*maggid*)
cup filled 125
forgot to recline 129
intention before drinking 129
Second seder
basic laws 149
eating matzo without intention 132
matzo 98
Seder
barech 141
chad gadya 147
children 115
exquisite items 111
great significance 113
hallel 144
kadesh 116
karpas 120
korech 135
maggid 123
main mitzvos 114
maror 133
motzi, matzo 130
nirtzah 147
Pesach on Sunday 155

reciting Haggadah in English 124
roasted meat 110, 137
rochtza 129
second seder in *chutz la'aretz* 149
Shir Hashirim 147
shulchan orech 136
stay up the whole night 148
tzafun 138
urchatz 119
wearing *kittel* 110
women's obligation 114
yachatz 122
Seder plate
arrangement 103
charoses 105
chazeres 104
egg 104
karpas 106
maror 104
roast meat 104
Self-cleaning oven
kashering 33
Selling chometz
a rented house 71
by telephone 70
definite chometz 66
different time zones 70
dried flowers 68
everyone should sell..... 68
flour 67
origin 66
Pesach on Sunday 151
pots 68
specify location 69
stocks 69
storing during Pesach ... 69
via an agent 70
Shabbos *Hagadol*
Haggadah recited 22
origin and significance .. 21
sermon delivered 22
Shabbos kettle
kashering 36

Index

Shampoo
   using 55
Shir Hashirim
   significance 147
***Shmura* matzo**
   hand-ground flour 97
   made by machine 97
   using at the seder 96
   using the entire Pesach . 97
Shoe polish
   using 55
Shopping
   precautions 53
Sink
   kashering 36, 37
Sink faucets
   kashering 37
Sink spout
   kashering 37
Soap
   using 55
Spilling wine
   drinking spilled wine ... 128
   how 127
Supervision
   canned fruits 51
   cosmetics 57
   dried fruits 51
   eye drops 56
   flavored lipstick 57
   frozen vegetables 51
   herbs 52
   medicinal creams 56
   medicine 56
   milk 51
   paperware 59
   perfume 58
   petroleum jelly 56
   plasticware 59
   salt 50
   sugar 50
   toothpaste 58
   vitamins 57
Table
   cleaning 26
Tablecloths
   cleaning 28
Third cup (*barech*)
   cup filled 141
   forgot to recline 142
   intention before drinking 142
Toaster
   put away 40
Toothpaste
   using 58
Toys
   cleaning 25
Tzafun
   meaning 138
Urchatz
   origin and significance . 119
   who washes 119
Vegetables
   peeling 52
   supervision of frozen vegetables 51
Ventilator
   covering 34
Vitamins
   taking 57
Wine
   carbonated 93
   forgot to recline . 118, 129, 142, 146
   holding during seder .. 142, 144
   holding during seder .. 116, 129
   intention before drinking first cup 117
   intention before drinking fourth cup 146
   intention before drinking second cup 129
   intention before drinking third cup 142
   open bottles before Yom Tov 112
   poured by another person 96
   red 93
   shmitta 96

spilling during *maggid*. 127
switching during seder .. 94
Women
  bedikas chometz 74
  hallel 144
  nullification of chometz . 85
  obligation in mitzvos of the seder 114
  reclining 107

repeating *shehecheyanu b'racha* 117
saying amen to *shehecheyanu b'racha* 117
Yachatz
  origin and significance . 122
Ze'roa
  on seder plate 104

Hebrew Sources

ראשי תיבות
יבק"ת: שו"ת יבקש תורה ח"ו להג"ר יצחק קויפמן, תשס"ב.
סה"פ: ספר הלכות פסח להג"ר שמעון איידער, 1998.
ספ"כ: סידור פסח כהלכתו להג"ר שלמה זלמן גרוסמן, ח"א תשנ"ג, ח"ב תשס"ב.

פרק א - חודש ניסן

[1] רמב"ן שמות פי"ב פ"ב, ר"ה יא/ב, רבינו בחיי שמות פי"ג פ"ד. [2] שבת פז/ב. [3] ס' תכט סע' ב וברמ"א, מ"ב ס"ק ח, רמ"א סו"ס רפד ומ"ב ס"ק יח. [4] מ"ב ס' תעא ס"ק יב, באר היטב סק"ה, חק יעקב סק"ז, אג"מ ח"א ס' קנה ד"ה ולמדה. [5] ס' תכט סע' ב ברמ"א, מ"ב סק"י, יא. [6] גשר החיים פכ"ט סע' ה, תשובות והנהגות ח"ב ס' סה. [7] ס' תכט סע' א ברמ"א. [8] מ"ב סק"ה. [9] מ"ב סק"ו, שעה"צ סק"י. [10] שיטה מקובצת ברכות מג/ב ד"ה האי מאן דנפיק, א"ר סדר הברכות סק"א, ערוה"ש סק"ב. [11] ס' רכו. [12] מ"ב סק"ב. [13] הגהות רע"א מסתפק, אבל כה"ח ס"ק יא כתב בשם האחרונים שאין לברך וע"ע הליכות שלמה פכ"ג הע' 120. [14] תשובות והנהגות ח"א ס' קצב, כה"ח הנ"ל. [15] סתימת הפוסקים שלא הזכירו שאין לברך על אילן א', וכן מביא בשו"ת ציץ אליעזר חי"ב ס' כ בס"ד, ובכה"ח סק"ב כ' שלכתחילה יש לחזר על מקום שיש בו ריבוי אילנות. [16] מ"ב סק"א, בה"ט סק"א, בצל החכמה ח"ו ס' לו, שו"ת הר צבי או"ח ח"א ס' קיח, וע' תשובות והנהגות ח"א ס' קצ, ציץ אליעזר שם, שערים מצויינים בהלכה סימן ס' סק"א. [17] כה"ח סק"ד, שו"ת בצל החכמה שם ס' לו, שו"ת ציץ אליעזר שם, תשובות והנהגות שם. [18] שו"ת הר צבי שם ושו"ת ציץ אליעזר שם. [19] שו"ת ציץ אליעזר שם. [20] מ"ב סק"ה. [21] מ"ב סק"ד, שעה"צ סק"ב, ג. [22] כה"ח סק"ז, שו"ת ציץ אליעזר שם. [23] שו"ת הר צבי שם, ציץ אליעזר שם, ותשובות והנהגות שם. [24] ס' תל, מ"ב סק"א, מטה משה אות תקמב. [25] מ"ב ס' תכט סק"א, ב. [26] ס' תל ברמ"א, מ"ב סק"ב, וע"ע פעולת שכיר למעשה רב אות קעז (ג).

פרק ב - ניקוי הבית

[הקדמה] מ"ב ס' תמב ס"ק כח, ס' תמה סק"ח, וע' דברים פכ"ח, פמ"ז. [27] שמות פי"ג פ"ז, פי"ב פט"ו, מ"ב ס' תלא סק"ב. [28] מ"ב ס' תמב ס"ק לג ושעה"צ ס"ק נב, חזו"א ס' קטז ס"ק יג ד"ה והגר"א, אג"מ ח"א ס' קמה, וע' יבק"ת ס' ט בסופו. [29] אלו אינם מקומות שמתכנסים בהם חמץ כמבואר בס' תלג סע' ג, ואפי' אם נתגלגל לשם מהני ביטול כמבואר בסע' ז ובמ"ב ס"ק כט וכן מבואר בגר"ז ס"ק יט. [30] מבקשי תורה אור אפרים פסקי הגרשז"א ענף

ב אות ז, ספ״כ פי״ג אות יד והע׳ 43, סה״פ פ״ו הע׳ סח בשם הגרמ״פ. [31] ספ״כ שם, סה״פ פ״ו D 6. [32] פשוט. [33] ימי הפסח עמ׳ כח בשם הגר״נ קרליץ, וכן שמעתי מהגר״י קויפמן בשם הגרי״ש״א. [34] סה״פ שם אות 7 והע׳ עב, ספ״כ פ״ח סע׳ כה אות 2, 3. [35] סה״פ שם ופט״ז C 1, ספ״כ שם, מבית לוי עמ׳ לח אות י. [36] סה״פ שם. [37] פשוט. [38] פשוט. [39] פשוט, וע׳ ספ״כ שאם שמים עליו אוכל חם צריך הכשר ע״י ערוי בכלי ראשון. [40] פשוט, וי״א שעדיף להסתירו. [41] ספ״כ פי״ג הע׳ 39 ע״פ מג״א ס׳ תמד סק״ו ועוד, ס׳ הכשרות פ״ו סע׳ ל, לא בשם החזו״א ובעל הקהלות יעקב. [42] סה״פ פט״ז B 6 בשם הגרמ״פ. [43] ספ״כ פ״ח סע׳ לט ובהע׳ 141, ס׳ הכשרות פ״ו סע׳ פב בשם הגרצ״פ פרנק, פסקי תשובות ס׳ תנא הע׳ 303 בשם מדריכי כשרות. [44] שו״ת מלמד להועיל ח״א ס׳ צג, דרכי תשובה ס׳ פט ס״ק יא, שו״ת מהרש״ם ח״א ס׳ קצז, שו״ת שבט הלוי ח״א ס׳ קמח, סה״פ פט״ז 6B, שערים מצויינים בהלכה סי׳ קטז סק״ד, וע׳ ספ״כ פ״ח סע׳ לד ובהערה שם, ספר הגעלת כלים פי״ג אות תלד* הע׳ שצח. [45] פשוט. [46] ס׳ הכשרות פ״ו סע׳ לד בשם קובץ מבית לוי ניסן. [47] פשוט. [48] ס׳ תלו סע׳ א, מ״ב סוף הסימן, פסקי תשובות אות ב, מבית לוי ניסן עמ׳ כה אות ב, הגדת מועז״ז (תשל״ד) עמ׳ קמז, וע״ע יבק״ס ט׳ ז. [49] ס׳ תלז.

פרק ג - הכשרת המטבח

[50] ס׳ תמז סע׳ א. [51] מ״ב ס׳ תנא סק״ב וס״ק קטו. [52] ס׳ תנא סע׳ ב, וע׳ סה״פ פט״ז הע׳ קמב שיש כמה פוסקים שמתירים להכשיר בליבון קל ובכללם יסודי ישורון והגר״א קוטלר, ויש מחמירים להצריך ליבון חמור וכן דעת הגרמ״פ וכן נפסק בשערים מצויינים בהלכה סי׳ קטז סק״ד שמתיר הכשר ע״י ליבון חמור, וע׳ ספ״כ פ״ח סע׳ לד ובהערה 7. [53] ע׳ במקורות 52. ומ״ש שעדיף לאפות לפני פסח, משום שאפ׳ את״ל שלא הוכשר כדין ונשאר משהו חמץ בתנור מ״מ חמץ בטל בששים לפני פסח, ע׳ ס׳ תמז סע׳ ב. [54] ספ״כ פ״ח אות ג ד, ספר הכשרות פ״א הע׳ צז, סה״פ פט״ז 4 E. [55] אגרות משה או״ח ח״א סו״ס קבד, סה״פ פט״ז 1D, ספ״כ פ״ח אות ד 1, ס׳ בכשרות פ״ו סע׳ יג, מבית לוי ניסן עמ׳ לו אות ג. [56] ספ״כ פ״ח אות ד 3, מבית לוי ניסן עמוד לו. [57] ספ״כ פ״ח אות ד 2, סה״פ פט״ז אות 2. [58] ספ״כ פ״ח ד 4, ספר הכשרות פ״ו הע׳ מו בס״ד. [59] ס׳ הכשרות פ״ו סע׳ טז, דקיי״ל לעניין חמץ ריחא מילתא - מ״ב ס׳ תמז ס״ק יג. [60] סה״פ פט״ז 1 D. [61] אג״מ ח״א סו״ס קבד, ספ״כ פ״ח סע׳ ה. [62] סה״פ פט״ז 6 E בשם הגרמ״פ דאמרי׳ כבולעו כך פולטו, ספר הכשרות פ״א הע׳ קה, וע״ע תשובות והנהגות ח״א ס׳ ריב שאין אומרים כבולעו כך פולטו בזיעה, וכן סובר הגר״ש ואזנר בקונ׳ מבית לוי ניסן עמ׳ לז. [63]

Hebrew Sources

מבית לוי ניסן עמ' לז אות ה, יבק"ת ס' יח אות י והטעם דלא מהני ליבון משום דילמא חייס, וע"ע סה"פ פט"ז 3 D, ספ"כ פ"ח אות ד. [64] סה"פ פט"ז 7 C. [65] מבית לוי ניסן עמ' מב אות ז. [66] רמ"א סימן תנא סע' ו, מ"ב סק"נ ומ"א, וס' תנב סק"א, שעה"צ ס' תמד סק"ד, סה"פ פט"ז C 5a. [67] סה"פ פט"ז 5 C, מבית לוי ניסן עמ' לד אות א, ספר הגעלת כלים פי"ג אות קכו בשם הגרי"י וייס. [68] סה"פ פט"ז 5 C, מבית לוי ניסן עמ' לה אות א. [69] סה"פ פט"ז 5 C, מבית לוי ניסן שם. [70] סה"פ פט"ז 5 C, מבית לוי ניסן שם. [71] מבית לוי ניסן שם, שעה"צ ס' תמד סק"ד. [72] ספ"כ פ"ח אות כב. [73] סה"פ פט"ז 4 C, ספ"כ פ"ח אות ט, ספר הכשרות פ"ו סע' יט. [74] ספר הכשרות שם הערה נה. [75] ספר הכשרות שם סע' כא והערה נט, ספ"כ פ"ח אות ט. [76] סה"פ פט"ז C 4. [77] שם. [78] רמ"א ס' תנג סע' א, מ"ב ס' תמב סוף סק"א, ספר הכשרות פ"ו הע' נט. [79] שעה"צ ס' תמח סק"כ, ספר הכשרות פ"ו הע' נט. [80] ספ"כ פ"ח אות ח 5, סה"פ פט"ז C 9, מבית לוי ניסן עמ' לח אות ט. [81] ס' הכשרות פ"ו סע' מא. [82] ס' תנא סע' ח, וע' מקורות 66, ספר הכשרות פ"ו סע' א ב, סה"פ פט"ז C 1, ספ"כ פ"ח אות ב. [83] ספק הכשרות שם סע' ד, מבית לוי ניסן עמ' לו אות ב, וע' ס' תמב סע' ו ומ"א ס"ק כח. [84] ספר הכשרות פ"ו סע' י, סה"פ פט"ז C 3, וע' ס' תנא מ"ב ס"ק קטו. [85] ספר הכשרות שם סע' יא. [86] ע' פסקי תשובות ס' תנא הע' 19, ספר הכשרות פ"ו סע' מא וה"ה להרבה כלים. [87] ס' תנא סע' א ומ"ב סק"ז, ספ"כ פי"א סע' יז.

פרק ד - הכשרת כלים

[88] מ"ב ס' תנא ס"ק יט, ס' תנב סק"ח, מבית לוי ניסן עמ' מא, יבק"ת ח"ו סי' יח אות ד (השנייה). [89] מ"ב ס' תנא ס"ק כח וס"ק פט. [90] סע' ד, ה, מבית לוי ניסן עמ' מב סע' ה. [91] סע' ד, רמ"א סע' י"א, ספ"כ פ"ט סע' יד. [92] מ"ב ס' תנב סק"ח, קצשו"ע ס' קטז סע' יח. [93] ס' תנא סע' ח, וע' ספ"כ פ"ט סע' ט באריכות. [94] סע' א, רמ"א סע' כו, חת"ס יו"ד ס' קיג הובא במ"ב על סע' כג, ספ"כ פ"ח סע' מ, ופ"ט באריכות (סע' ח, יא, טז, כה ועוד). [95] מ"ב ס"ק כב, גר"ז ס"ק טו. [96] מ"ב ס"ק כג, שעה"צ ס"ק כו. [97] שם. [98] רמ"א סע' יח. [99] מבית לוי ניסן עמ' מא סע' ג. [100] ע' מקורות 65. [101] סע' יד, מ"ב ס"ק פא. [102] רמ"א ס' תנב סע' ב. [103] ס' תנב סע' ג, מ"ב שם, סה"פ פט"ו B 2d. [104] סה"פ פי"ב B 4. [105] ע' ס' תלז סע' ד, וזה רק כשכבר עבר עליו מעל"ע, שההגעלה אינו אלא מדרבנן. [106] ס' הכשרות פ"ג סע' ו בשם שו"ת ציץ אליעזר ס' חי"ב ס' נה. [107] שם סע' ז בשם שו"ת משנה הלכות ח"י ס' קז. [108] מ"ב ס' תנא ס"ק יט.

פרק ה - השגחה לפסח

[109] כך ביררנו ממשגיחי כשרות. [110] פשוט. [111] מדריך כשרות לבד"ץ העדה החרדית תשס"ב עמ' מד. [112] מ"ב ס' תסז ס"ק כו, כך ביררנו ממשגיחי כשרות. [113] כך ביררנו ממשגיחי כשרות. [114] שם. [115] מ"ב ס' תסז ס"ק לד, וזה מקור המנהג לא להשתמש בהם להבדלה. [116] חיי"א כלל קבו סע' ז. [117] כך ביררנו ממשגיחי כשרות, מ"ב ס' תמח ס"ק לג. [118] חמץ משהו עמ' 101, ס' הכשרות עמ' שנד, שס. [119] כך ביררנו ממשגיחי כשרות. [120] פסקי תשובות ס' תסז אות יא והע' 55. [121] ס' הכשרות פ"י סע' עב, עג, עח. [122] ס' תמז מ"ב ס"ק פה, פו. [123] ביה"ל ריש סי' תמג, ספ"כ פ"י סע' יא, תשובות והנהגות ח"ד ס' צז אות ו' וע' ש"ך יו"ד סו"ס קמב.

פרק ו - חמץ בפסח

[124] ס' תמב, מ"ב ס"ק לט, מג. [125] מ"ב ס"ק מג. [126] אג"מ או"ח ח"ג ס' סב. [127] מדריך כשרות לבד"ץ העדה החרדית עמ' נה. [128] שם עמ' סב. [129] חזו"א ס' קטז סע' ח, אג"מ או"ח ח"ב ס' צב, יבק"ת ס' י, וע"ע באחיעזר ח"ג ס' לג אות ד שיש איסור אחשביה בתרופות. [130] שש"כ פ"מ סע' עד, ספר הכשרות פכ"א הע' קנו בשם הגרשז"א, וקטע ד"ה אמנם, מנחת שלמה ח"א סי' יז. [131] מדריך כשרות לבד"ץ העדה החרדית עמ' סב. [132] ספר הכשרות פכ"א סע' עג, פסקי תשובות ס' תמב הע' 24, סה"פ פ"ב C 4. [133] סה"פ פ"ב C 11. [134] סה"פ שם, ספר הכשרות פכ"א הע' קע. [135] סה"פ שם. [136] אג"מ ח"ג ס' סב, מקראי קודש ח"א ס' נד, ספר הכשרות פכ"א סע' עה והע' קע בשם כמה פוסקים ובכללם הגרח"פ שייינברג, וע' יבק"ת ס' י באריכות. [137] סה"פ פ"ב C 10. [138] סה"פ פ"ב C 12 בשם הגרמ"פ והגר"א קוטלר. [139] סה"פ פ"ב C 12. [140] כך ביררנו ממשגיחי כשרות. [141] סה"פ פ"ג B 9. [142] שם.

פרק ז - קטניות

[143] רמב"ם הל' כלאים פ"א ה"ח, ספ"כ פט"ז סע' ג. [144] ס' תנג מ"ב סק"ו וביה"ל שם. [145] מנח"י ח"ג ס' קלח, אג"מ ח"ג ס' סג. [146] מקראי קודש ח"ב ס' ס אות ב בשם הגר"ח סאלאוויייצ'יק, מנח"י ח"ג ס' קלח, ספ"כ פט"ז הע' 26 בשם הגרמ"פ, יבק"ת ס' יט. [147] מ"ב ס"ק ז. [148] שם. [149] מהר"ם שי"ק ס' רמא, שו"ת זרע אמת ח"ב ס' מח, מהרלנ"ח ס' קכא הובא בכה"ח ס' תנג, סע' כז. [150] ספ"כ פט"ז סע' ו, מבית לוי ח"ז עמ' יח. [151] מ"ב ס' תנג סק"ט, ספ"כ פט"ז סע' ו, ט. [152] ספ"כ פט"ז סע' ט והע' 37, כי טעם הקטניות בטל בתבשיל, ע' מ"ב סק"ח. [153] חק יעקב ס' תעא ס"ק ב וספ"כ פט"ז הע' 42*

Hebrew Sources

[154] בשם הגריש"א. [155] סע' א בהג"ה ומ"ב ס"ק יב. [156] סע' א בהג"ה, ספ"כ פט"ז סע' ז והע' 34. ע' מקורות 78.

פרק ח - שרויה (ס' תנח)

[157] מ"ב סק"ד. [158] שע"ת ס' תנט וס' תס. [159] מ"ב שם, שו"ת גר"ז סי' ו. [160] אג"מ ח"ג ס' סד. [161] שערים מצויינים בהלכה ס' קיג סק"ז. [162] שמעתי מהגר"ז ובר.

פרק ט - מכירת חמץ (ס' תמח)

[163] סע' ג, מ"ב ס"ק יב. [164] ערוה"ש ס"ק כז, סה"פ פי"א A 9. [165] סה"פ פי"א A 9 הע' מד בשם הגרמ"פ, יבק"ת ס' יג, מעשה רב אות קפ, סע' ג, מבית לוי ניסן עמ' כו אות י"ב, א"ר סק"ז, ב"ח. [166] מבית לוי ניסן שם והערה ה'. [167] מדריך כשרות לבד"ץ העדה החרדית תשס"ב עמ' מה. [168] תשובות והנהגות ח"א ס' שט, חג בחג פ"י הע' 16. [169] מדריך כשרות לבד"ץ העדה החרדית שם. [170] סה"פ פי"א סוף אות A. [171] קצש"ע ס' קיד סע' ג, שו"ת חת"ס ס' קט בשם ר' נתן אדלר, מבית לוי ניסן עמ' כו אות יג. [172] מבית לוי ח"ז עמ' טז. [173] מנח"י ח"ג סי' א, מועדים וזמנים ח"ג ס' רסט (א), וע"ע שו"ת חשב האפוד ח"א ס' סב. [174] אג"מ ח"א ס' קנ. [175] מ"ב ס"ק יב. [176] שם. [177] אג"מ ח"א ס' קנ, ספ"כ פי"א סע' יח. [178] ספ"כ פי"א סע' ט. [179] ספ"כ פי"א סע' י בשם הגריש"א והגר"נ קרליץ. [180] תשובות והנהגות ח"ב ס' ריח. [181] ע' אג"מ ח"ד ס' צד/צה, מנח"י ח"ז ס' כה. [182] מבית לוי ניסן עמ' כה אות ה.

פרק י - בדיקת חמץ (ס' תלא)

[183] סע' א. [184] פשוט, וע' ס' תלה ומ"ב סק"ב. [185] מ"ב ס"ק ח. [186] מ"ב שם, הליכות שלמה פ"א הערה 62, אג"מ ח"ד ס' צט. [187] מ"ב סק"א. [188] סע' ב, מ"ב סק"ה, יב. [189] מ"ב ס"ק ה. [190] מ"ב סק"ז שעה"צ סק"ז. [191] סע' ב, מ"ב סק"ו. [192] מ"ב ס' תרעב סק"י, ס' רלה ס"ק יז. [193] ע' מבית לוי ח"י עמ' כב לגבי נר חנוכה, ופשוט דה"ה כאן. [194] ס' תלב סע' א. [195] שם. [196] מ"ב סק"ד. [197] מ"ב סק"ח. [198] סע' ב, מ"ב סק"ט. [199] מ"ב ס"קי, וסק"ח. [200] מ"ב סק"ג. [201] סע' א, מ"ב סק"ה. [202] מ"ב סק"ו, סע' א. [203] סע' ב. [204] כה"ח ס"ק כב. [205] מבית לוי ניסן עמ' לא אות ט. [206] מבקשי תורה אור אפרים, פסקי הגרשז"א, ענף ב אות א. [207] ס' תלא סע' א, ס' תלג סע' ג מ"ב סק"י יט, כה"ח ס"ק ל. [208] מ"ב ס' תלו ס"ק לב. [209] שע"ת סו"ס תלג, שעה"צ ס' תלב ס"ק יב, שעה"צ ס' תלג ס"ק נו, מבית לוי ניסן עמ' לא סע' יא, יבק"ת ס' ד. [210] ס' תלב סע' ב, שעה"צ ס"ק יב. [211] שע"ת ס' תלב סק"ג. [212] שם. [213] מבקשי תורה אור אפרים, פסקי הגרשז"א ענף ב אות ג, ולגבי ארון בגדים, ע' ס' תלג סע' ב, וה"ה כאן, שערים מצויינים

בהלכה ס' קיא סק"ד, וע' מ"ב ס' תלג סק"ח. [214] מבקשי תורה שם אות ד, מבית לוי ניסן עמ' ל' הע' ח. [215] ס' תלד סע' ב, סה"פ פ"ז 3 A והערה ט. [216] פשוט. [217] רמ"א שם, מ"ב סק"ט, ספ"כ פי"ג סע' יז. [218] עיין מקורות 49. [219] ס' תלו סע' א מ"ב סק"ג, מנח"י ח"ח ס' לה. [220] מבית לוי ניסן עמ' לג, שו"ת ח"ד ס' מד. [221] מבית לוי שם, שו"ת מהרש"ם ח"ג ס' רצא, תשובות והנהגות ח"ב ס' ריא (ג). [222] מבית לוי עמ' לג אות יג, ספ"כ פי"ג סע' ט.

פרק יא - ערב פסח

[223] רמ"א ס' תכט סע' ב, מ"ב ס"ק יג. [224] ס' תמג סע' א, מ"ב סק"ח, מבית לוי ניסן עמ' נד אות א. [225] רמ"א ס' תמה סע' א, מ"ב ס' תלג ס"ק כח. [226] מ"ב ס' תמה סק"ז. [227] ספ"כ פט"ו סע' ד ע"פ רמ"א ריש סי' תמה. [228] שם, מ"ב ס' תמה סק"א, מבית לוי ניסן עמ' נד אות ג. [229] מ"ב סק"ז. [230] מ"ב סק"ה. [231] ס' תלד סע' ב ורמ"א, מ"ב סק"ט, ס' תלג סק"ז מז. [232] מ"ב ס' תלד סק"ק יא, דע"ת ס' תלד סוס"ע ג. [233] ס' תלד סע' ב מ"ב סק"ק יב. [234] ימי הפסח עמ' קמא בשם הגרב"צ פלמן, הלכות חג בחג פ"ח הי"ד. [235] ס' תסח סע' א, מ"ב סק"א, ב, ז. [236] מ"ב סק"ה. [237] שם. [238] מ"ב סק"ז, ואין איסור אם גומרת לבד, שאינו חמור מן ער"ש. [239] ארחות רבינו ח"ב עמ' נו. [240] מבית לוי ניסן עמ' נד אות ט, ארחות רבינו ח"ב עמ' נו. [241] מבית לוי שם. [242] רמ"א ס' תסח סע' ב, מ"ב סק"ח. [243] רמב"ם חו"מ פ"י הי"ב, תפא"י פ"י אות ג, ס' תעא מג"א סק"ו. [244] רמ"א ס' תעא סע' ב, מ"ב ס"ק יג. [245] ספ"כ פט"ו סע' יד, שבה"ל ח"ח ס' קיז שאלה א, פסקי הגרשז"א הובא במבקשי תורה ענף ז אות ד. [246] מ"ב ס' תעא סק"כ, חיי"א כלל קבט סע' יג. [247] עיין מקורות 153. [248] ס' תעא סע' א, מ"ב סק"ג. [249] לוח א"י, מעשה רב אות קצ, מ"ב ס' תעא ס"ק כב. [250] רמב"ם טומאת אוכלים פט"ז ה"י, מ"ב ס' קכח ס"ק קסה, חיי"א כלל עט סע' א, מ"ב ס' תעא סק"ק כב. [251] מ"ב שם, כה"ח ס' תסח ס"ק קא.

פרק יב - תענית בכורים (ס' תע)

[252] סע' א, ב. [253] ס' תקסד. [254] מ"ב סק"א. [255] מ"ב סק"ב, ד. [256] מבית לוי ניסן עמ' נ אות ב. [257] חק יעקב סק"ב, כה"ח סק"ג. [258] רמ"א סע' ב, מ"ב סק"ט, י, ערוה"ש סק"ד. [259] מ"ב סק"י. [260] ספ"כ פי"ד הע' 14, מנח"י ח"ט ס' מה, תשובות והנהגות ח"ב ס' רי. [261] מבית לוי עמ' נא אות ז. [262] מנח"י שם, ספ"כ פי"ד סע' 13*. [263] ספ"כ פי"ד סע' ו, אג"מ ח"א ס' קנז, שו"ת משנה הלכות ח"ו ס' קסו. [264] מנח"י

ח"ב ס' צג. [265] ספ"כ פי"ד סע' ח. [266] שו"ת בצל החכמה ח"ד סי' ק. [267] מ"ב סק"ב. [268] מבית לוי ניסן עמ' נא אות ח.

פרק יג - הכנות לסדר (ס' תעב)

[269] פסחים קיז סוף עמ' ב, רשב"ם צט/ב ד"ה ולא יפחתו לו. [270] ס' תעב סע' יא, מ"ב סק"ב לח, מבית לוי ניסן עמ' נט אות ז, מ"ב ס' שכ סק"י נו. [271] מבית לוי ניסן עמ' נח אות ה. [272] סע' י, מ"ב סק"י לה, לז, כה"ח סק"ח עב. [273] קול דודי פ"ג אות ד בשם הגרמ"פ, הגדת הלילה הזה ח"א עמ' 11 בשם הגריש"א. [274] מ"ב ס' קעה סק"ב, הסדר הערוך פי"ד אות י"ד. [275] מ"ב סק"ק לז. [276] ביה"ל ס' רעא סע' יג, ד"ה של רביעית. [277] מ"ב סק"ל. [278] מחה"ש סק"ק יא בשם הב"ח, שעה"צ ס' רי סק"ק יא, מ"ב ס' תעב סק"ק לד. [279] פסקי תשובות אות ז. [280] רמ"א ס' תעג סע' א, מבית לוי ניסן עמ' עא. [281] שמות פי"ב פי"ז, ס' תנג סע"ד. [282] מ"ב ס' תנג סק"ק כא. [283] מקראי קודש ח"ב ס' ג, יבק"ת ס' כ. [284] ביה"ל ריש סי' תס, וע' יבק"ת ס' כא. [285] מ"ב ס' תס סק"ק ב, ערוה"ש סק"כ. [286] רמב"ם חו"מ פ"ו ה"א, שיעורי תורה ס' ג סע' יב, שיעורין של תורה שיעורי המצוות אות כד. [287] מ"ב ס' תפו סק"ק א. [288] ס' תעה סע' א, מ"ב סק"ק טז, ס' תעז סע' א מ"ב סק"ק א, ס' תפו סע' א ומ"ב סק"ק א. [289] מנחת חינוך מצוה ו' ומצוה י', מצות מצוה פי"ב הכ"ג. [290] פשוט. [291] סי' שו סע' ז, ששכ"כ פכ"ט סע' לח. [292] מ"ב ס' תנד סק"ק טו, צי"א חי"א ס' טו אות ח, ט. [293] מ"ב ס' תעג סק"ק לד, כה"ח סק"ח עב. [294] מ"ב ס' סק"ק מב. [295] מ"ב שם, גר"ז סק"ל, חיי"א כלל קל סק"ג, הגהות חת"ס לסע' ה, והחזו"א הקפיד שיהיה מר, ע' ס' קכד דף לט/א. [296] מ"ב סק"ק לח. [297] מ"ב סק"ק לו, ספ"כ ח"ב פ"ט סע' ד. [298] ס' תקד סע' ג, מ"ב סק"ק יט, ספ"כ שם. [299] מ"ב ס' תעג סק"ק מו. [300] ס' תעג סע' ד, ערוה"ש סע' יא, כה"ח סק"ק נח. [301] רמ"א סוס"י תעה. [302] באה"ט סק"ח, ערוה"ש שם. [303] פשוט, וע' כה"ח הנ"ל שכן צריך לעשות לכתחילה. [304] מ"ב סק"ק יז. [305] באה"ט סק"ח, חיי"א כלל קל הסדר בקצרה ס"ק יא. [306] סע' ד, מ"ב ס"ק כז, לב. [307] כה"ח ס' תעג סק"ס, וע' סדר הערוך פי"ט סע' ד שהמקור לקחת צואר העוף מרש"י בס' האורה שכ' שהיו נתפחים מפרקותיהם של ישראל מהחומר הכבד שעל כתפיהם, פרמ"ג א"א סק"ז. [308] מ"ב סק"ק לב. [309] מ"ב סק"ק כג. [310] סע' ד וברמ"א, מ"ב ס"ק לב. [311] ויגד משה ס' ג אות י. [312] מ"ב ס' תעו ס"ק יא, ס' תעג ס"ק לב. [313] רמ"א ס' תעג סע' ה. [314] שם, הסדר הערוך פי"ח סע' ד. [315] מ"ב ס"ק מז, ס' שכ"א ס"ק סח. [316] קיצש"ע ס' קיח סע' ב, ערוה"ש ס' תעג סק"י. [317] רמב"ם הל' חו"מ פ"ז הל' ו, ז. [318] רמ"א ס' תעב סע' ד, מועו"ז ח"ג ס' רנז.

[319] מועו"ז שם, שמע בני עמ' 63 בשם הגרח"פ שיינברג. [320] מ"ב ס' תעב ס"ק יג. [321] מ"ב ס"ק טו, טז, מבית לוי ניסן עמ' ע. [322] סע' ה. [323] מ"ב סק"ז, ומש"כ שם תחת ראשו אמר הגרח"ק שלא נהגו כן. [324] מ"ב סק"ח. [325] שם. [326] סע' ג, מ"ב סק"ט. [327] מ"ב סק"י. [328] רמ"א סע' ג, מ"ב ס"ק יא. [329] מ"ב שם, פר"ח סק"ג. [330] כה"ח ס"ק כב. [331] ס' תעב סע' ז, ס' תעה סע' א, ס' תעז סע' א. [332] מ"ב ס' תעג ס"ק עא. [333] ס' תעו סע' א. [334] מ"ב סק"א. [335] רמ"א ס' תרי סע' ד, ט"ז ס' תעב סק"ג. [336] כן נהגו. [337] מ"ב ס"ק יג. [338] פסקי תשובות הע' 14 בשם הגריש"א. [339] ס' תעב סע' ב, מ"ב סק"ו, הסדר הערוך פי"ג סע' ז, ועי' תרגום יונתן בן עוזיאל בראשית פכ"ז פ"א, ובעל הטורים שם פסוק כז. [340] סע' א, מ"ב סק"א, גר"ז סע' לא.

פרק יד - הסדר

[341] מהרי"ל ריש הלכות סדר ההגדה. [342] יסוד ושורש העבודה שער ט', ריש פ"ו. [343] רמב"ם חו"מ פ"ו ה"א, פ"ז ה"א, ז, י, יב. [344] ס' תעג סע' ד, ס' תעב סע' ב, ט"ז. [345] ויגד משה ס' ט אות ז, תרגום יונתן בן עוזיאל בראשית פכ"ז פ"א. [346] ס' תעב סע' יד, מ"ב ס"ק מד. [347] ס' תעב סע' טו מ"ב ס"ק מז, מ"ב ס' תפו סק"א, מ"ב ס' תעב סע' טז ס"ק נ. [348] רמ"א סו"ס תעג, מ"ב ס"ק עח. [349] ויגד משה ס' טו אות ו, י, ספ"כ ח"ג פ"ג סע' ו. [350] שש"כ פמ"ז ס"ק כו. [351] מבית לוי ניסן עמ' עא והע' טז, ספ"כ ח"ב פ"ג סע' ו. [352] שם, שמעתי מהגרא"צ. [353] מ"ב ס' תעג סק"א, כה"ח סק"ו, אבודרהם (סדר תפילות של חול, שער שלישי לבאר בו ברכת המצות ומשפטיהם ד"ה ואם תאמר והרי), מ"ב ס' תעב ס"ק כא. [354] עיין מקורות 277. [355] עיין מקורות 278. [356] מ"ב ס' תעב ס"ק כא. [357] הלילה הזה עמ' 13 בשם הגריש"א. [358] מ"ב ס' תעג ס"ק טז, גר"ז ס"ק יג, מ"ב ס' ר"ח ס"ק עב ושעה"צ ס"ק עא, ולעניין שאר משקין, יש חשש מוסיף על הכוסות אם מברך שהכל. [359] ס' תעג סע' ו, שעה"צ ס"ק סט, ועי' ט"ז סק"ו, מ"ב ס' קנח סק"כ. [360] ספ"כ ח"ב פ"ד סע' א והע' 2, מבית לוי ניסן עמ' עב, ויגד משה ס' טז אות ה. [361] ספ"כ שם הע' 3. [362] ספ"כ ח"ב פ"ד סע' א, פסקי תשובות ס' תעג סע' 121 בשם הגרשז"א. [363] ספ"כ ח"ב פ"ד סע' ג. [364] מ"ב ס' תעג ס"ק יט, כא. [365] מ"ב ס"ק כא, ב"ח ד"ה ולוקח, רבינו מנוח על הרמב"ם פ"ח ה"ב. [366] מבית לוי ניסן עמ' עג. [367] ס' תעג סע' ו. [368] מ"ב ס' קנח סק"ו, הלכות חג בחג עמ' תקכה. [369] מבית לוי ניסן עמ' עג, ועי' רמ"א ס' ריג סע' א ומ"ב ס"ק יב. [370] מ"ב ס"ק נה. [371] חג בחג עמ' תקכב, מבית לוי ניסן עמ' עג, קול דודי פ"ט אות ח. [372] כה"ח ס"ק נב. [373] מ"ב ס' תעג

Hebrew Sources

ס"ק נז. [374] מ"ב ס"ק נח, חק יעקב ס' תעה ס"ק כו בשם מהרי"ו. [375] הסדר הערוך פנ"ו סע' ז, ספ"כ ח"ב פ"ח סע' יא. [376] חק יעקב ס' תעב סק"ב. [377] ספר המצוות לרמב"ם מ"ע קנז. [378] רמ"א ס' תעג סע' ו, מ"ב ס"ק סג, סד. [379] מ"ב שם. [380] ע' מ"ב שם שכתב שאשה תכנס ותשמע וכו', וע' מעשה רב אות קצא שכ' "ואומר הגדה וכולם שומעים". [381] כה"ח ס"ק קכו, מ"ב סק"ס. [382] סע' ו ומ"ב ס"ק סו, סע' ז ומ"ב ס"ק סט, ביה"ל שם ד"ה הרשות בידו וכו'. [383] סע' ז. [384] מ"ב סק"ע. [385] סע' ז. [386] פשוט. [387] הלכות חג בחג עמ' תקלז ע"פ אוח"ה במדבר פ"ט, פי"ד. [388] עיין מקורות 332. [389] רמ"א סו"ס תעג. [390] מ"ב ס"ק עד, שעה"צ ס"ק פא, וע' ד"מ אות יח. [391] מהרי"ל סדר הגדה אות כז, כה"ח ס"ק קסח. [392] ויגד משה ס' כב אות יא. [393] קול דודי פי"א אות יב. [394] רמ"א סע' ז. [395] סע' ז. [396] מ"ב ס"ק עב, חק יעקב ס"ק לו. [397] עיין מקורות 317. [398] ס' תעג סע' ז, קול דודי פ' יא אות טז, ערוה"ש ס"ק כג. [399] מ"ב ס' קעד סק"ו. [400] מ"ב ס' תעב ס"ק כא. [401] ס' תעה סע' א, ביה"ל ד"ה יטול ידיו. [402] מ"ב ס"ק כד, ויגד משה ס' כד אות ח וס' כג אות ג. [403] חג בחג עמ' תקמז. [404] קול דודי פ' יג אות א. [405] ס' תעה סע' א, מ"ב סק"ו. [406] מ"ב סק"ב. [407] מ"ב סק"ג. [408] חג בחג פט"ז סע' ד, ויגד משה ס' כד אות כח, פסקי תשובות ס' תעה אות ב. [409] מ"ב סק"ד. [410] שיעורין של תורה שיעורי המצוות אות ל, חג בחג עמ' תקנ. [411] הלילה הזה עמ' 19 ע"פ מ"ב ס' תסא ס"ק יח. [412] מ"ב ס' תעב סק"ו כב. [413] מ"ב ס' תעה ס"ק לד, דקיי"ל מצוות א"צ כוונה בדרבנן, ע' מ"ב ס' ס סק"א. [414] הלילה הזה עמ' 265, ספ"כ ח"ב פ"ט סע' יא. [415] מ"ב ס' תעג סק"מ, מנהג ישראל תורה ח"ג עמ' קנ. [416] הלילה הזה עמ' 20. [417] מ"ב ס' תעה ס"ק יג, רמ"א ס' תעג סע' ה. [418] תוס' פסחים קטז/א ד"ה צריך, קול דודי ס' טו אות כג. [419] מ"ב ס' תעה ס"ק יג, וכן נוהגים. [420] רמ"א ס' ריג סע' א, ומ"ב ס"ק יב. [421] ס' תעה סע' פר"ח ד"ה ומ"ש כדי שתעלה, מ"ב ס"ק לד, הגש"פ חיים לראש. [422] מ"ב שם, גר"ז סע' כט. [423] מ"ב ס"ק יד. [424] תפא"י פסחים פ"י אות טו. [425] מ"ב ס' תעה ס"ק טז. [426] סע' א, ספ"כ ח"ב פ"ח סע' יד. [427] ע' מ"ב ס' תפו סק"א. [428] מ"ב ס"ק טז, וע' מקורות 414. [429] מ"ב ס"ק יט. [430] קיצשו"ע ס' קיט סע' ז, ערוה"ש ס' תעה סק"ז. [431] סע' א, ביה"ל ד"ה ואומר, קיצשו"ע ס' קיט סע' ז, גר"ז ס"ק יח. [432] הלילה הזה עמ' 21. [433] סע' א, מ"ב ס"ק כג. [434] גר"ז סע' ב. [435] רמ"א ס' תעו סע' ב, מ"ב ס"ק יא, ויגד משה ס' כז אות ה, מבית לוי ניסן עמ' סח. [436] עיין מקורות 309. [437] סדר הערוך פצ"ד סע' יב. [438] ס'

תעו סע' א, ורמ"א שם, ס' תעז סע' א. [439] רמ"א ס' תעב סע' ז, ויגד משה ס' כז אות יד. [440] ויגד משה ס' כז אות יג ד"ה והנה, ע"פ שו"ע ס' תקכט סע' א. [441] ימי הפסח עמ' קנד בשם הגר"נ קרליץ. [442] פסחים קיט/ב. [443] ס' תעז סע' א. [444] שם. [445] ס' תעז סע' א, מ"ב סק"א. [446] מ"ב שם. [447] מ"ב ס' תעה ס"ק לד, ס' מצות השם סדר אכילת הפסח. [448] ס' תעז סע' א. [449] מ"ב ס' תעז סק"ד, ס' תעב סק"ג כג, אג"מ ח"ג ס' סז. [450] ס' תעז סע' א, מ"ב סק"ו. [451] רמ"א סוף סע' ב. [452] סע' ב, מ"ב סק"ח, ט, יא, טז, יז. [453] ס' תעח סע' א, מ"ב סק"א. [454] מ"ב שם. [455] מ"ב סק"ב, ס' תפא סק"א, רמ"א סו"ס קצז, הלילה הזה עמ' 22. [456] ס' תעט סע' א, מ"ב סק"א. [457] סדר הערוך פ"ק סע' ד בשם לקט יושר עמ' לו ד"ה וזכורני, שבעל תרוה"ד נטל מי"א רק בליל הסדר. [458] רמ"א סו"ס תעט, מ"ב ס"ק יג. [459] מ"ב ס' ס, סק"י. [460] ויגד משה ס' כט אות ה, קול דודי פ' יט אות ו. [461] כה"ח ס' קפג ס"ק יט, קצה"ש ס' מו ס"ק כא. [462] ס' תעט סע' א. [463] רמ"א ס' תעב סע' ז. [464] ס' קפח סע' ו, תשובות והנהגות ח"א ס' שח. [465] ויגד משה סי' ל אות ג, ו. [466] ויגד משה שם אות ג, ד. [467] מ"ב ס' תפ סק"י, ספרים בשם הגר"א. [468] ויגד משה שם אות ה. [469] רמ"א סו"ס תפ. [470] ערוה"ש סק"א, ויגד משה סי' ל אות ח. [471] מ"ב סי' ס, סק"י. [472] ס' תעב סע' יד, ח"י ס"ק כז. [473] ויגד משה ס' לא אות ד ע"פ רש"י פסחים ל/א ד"ה שעונין עליו דברים. [474] ויגד משה שם אות ח, קול דודי פ' כ אות ד. [475] באה"ט סו"ס תעג. [476] רמ"א ס' תעט, מ"ב סק"ט. [477] מ"ב ס' תפ סק"ה. [478] שם. [479] מ"ב סי' ס, סק"י, ס' תעב סק"ל. [480] ס' תפ סע' א. [481] רמ"א ס' תעב סע' ז. [482] מ"ב ס' תעב סק"ל, ס' תעד סק"ג. [483] חג בחג עמ' תקסו. [484] מ"ב ס' רח ס"ק נח. [485] רמ"א ס' תעז סע' א, מ"ב סק"ז. [486] מ"ב ס' תפ סק"ו. [487] ויגד משה ס' לב אות ח, הגדת הגר"א. [488] חיי"א כלל קל הסדר בקצרה סע' טז. [489] ס' תפא סע' ב, חג בחג עמ' תקסו. [490] רמ"א סו"ס תפא, מ"ב סק"ד. [491] ע' רמ"א ס' תפא סע' ב ס' שכל הדינים שווים, ולעניין עריכת השלחן ע' פרמ"ג א"א ריש ס' תמד, ולעניין חצות ע' ויגד משה ס' כח אות יא, ולעניין שתיה ע' באה"ט ס' תפא סק"ג, ולעניין שינה ע' ויגד משה ס' לג אות ב. [492] יו"ט שני כהלכתו פ"ב סע' א. [493] שם פ"ג סע' כח, הע' פד בשם הגריש"א. [494] שם והערה פה.

פרק טו - פסח שחל במוצ"ש (ס' תמד)

[495] ס' תע סע' ב. [496] ס' תמד סע' א, מ"ב סק"א. [497] פסקי תשובות אות יז. [498] סע' ב, מ"ב סק"ט, י. [499] ביה"ל סע' א. [500] שע"ת סוף הסימן. [501] מ"ב ס' תעג ס"ק לח, ס' תקד ס"ק

יט. [502] מבית לוי חט"ז עמ' יח, מ"ב ס' תמד ס"ק כא, שש"כ פי"ל הע' קכא.   [503] ע' אג"מ ח"א ס' קנה ד"ה ולכן טוב שהתיר. ומבית לוי חט"ז עמ' כ אסר. ולמעשה אינו נוגע כ"כ שבזה"ז קשה להשיג מצה עשירה עם השגחה מעולה.   [504] רמ"א ס' תעא סע' ב ומ"ב ס"ק יד, מג"א סק"ו, אג"מ הנ"ל ד"ה נמצא שלמעשה. [505] מ"ב ס' תמד סק"ח, וס' רצא ס"ק טו, אגרות חזו"א ח"א ס' קפח.   [506] מ"ב ס"ק כב.   [507] מ"ב ס' רצ סק"ד.   [508] רמ"א ס' תמד סע' א, מ"ב סק"ח.   [509] מ"ב ס' רצט ס"ק לו.   [510] ס' תעג סע' א, מ"ב שם סק"ג, שש"כ פס"ב הע' כז בשם הגרשז"א, שו"ת באר משה ח"ו ס' קלו, ויגד משה ס' טו אות י, מבית לוי חט"ז עמ' כד.

פרק טז - חמץ אחר פסח

[511] ס' תמח סע' ג.   [512] ע' מקורות 165, מ"ב ס' תמט סק"ה. [513] פסקי תשובות ס' תמח הע' 44 בשם החזו"א והגריי"ק.   [514] שעה"צ ס' תסו סק"ד.

פרק יז - חדש

[515] יו"ד ס' רצג סע' א.   [516] שם, ש"ך סק"א.   [517] שם סע' ב, גר"א סק"ב.   [518] שם, ט"ז סק"ב.   [519] מ"ב ס' תפט ס"ק מה, רמ"א יו"ד שם סע' ג.   [520] מ"ב שם.   [521] פסקי תשובות ס' תפט אות ל, מדריך לחדש לר' יוסף הרמן.   [522] מדריך הנ"ל. [523] פשוט.

לע"נ

ר' חזקיהו יחיאל
ב"ר אפרים דוד ז"ל

נלב"ע א' מרחשון תשס"ג

ת.נ.צ.ב.ה.

לע"נ

ר' שמעון ב"ר משה הכהן ז"ל

נלב"ע י"א שבט תשי"ס

ר' גדליה דוד ב"ר איסר ז"ל

נלב"ע ז' תמוז תשל"ג

ר' פינחס ב"ר משה אהרן ז"ל

נלב"ע כ"ב שבט תשל"ט

ר' דוב אריה ב"ר משה צבי ז"ל

נלב"ע כ"א שבט תשנ"ז

ת. נ. צ. ב. ה.

Dedicated in loving memory of

ר' משה בן ר' הירש וואלף ז"ל

(Morris Kaiser)

נפטר כ"ד שבט תשנ"ט

ת.נ.צ.ב.ה.

לעילוי נשמת

האי גברא יקירא,
מוקיר רבנן,
קובע עיתים לתורה,
גומל צדקה וחסד,

הר״ר זישא אלכסנדר
בן ר' פינחס זצ״ל
פלוס

נלב״ע כ״ג בשבט תשנ״ח

ת.נ.צ.ב.ה.

לע"נ

ר' מאיר בן ר' חיים גלאט

נפטר ג' סיון תשס"ב

הונצח ע"י משפחתו

ת.נ.צ.ב.ה.

לע"נ

מרת מיכלא באבקא
בת ר' עזריאל זאב ע"ה

ת.נ.צ.ב.ה.

Dedicated for the Iluy Nishmas of
our loving Parents and Grandparents

יעקב בן משה ז״ל
עטא בת אילייעס ע״ה

May their memory be blessed

*Gedaliah and Chana Chassia Shofnos
and Family*

"To You alone we give thanks.
Even if our mouths were filled with song, like the sea
And our tongues with exultation like the roaring of its waves,
And our lips with praise like the breadth of the firmament,
And our eyes were radiant like the sun and the moon,
And our hands outspread like eagles of the sky,
And our feet light as the deer –
We would never sufficiently thank You, Hashem,
our G-d and G-d of our fathers,
And bless your name for even one thousandth of the
billions and trillions of favors…"

Dedicated to our children and grandchildren
that they may always thank and serve Hashem
with hearts full of love and gratitude.

Akiva and Hinde Gordon

In Loving Memory of

Edmond Rose
ר׳ חיים איסר
ב״ר מרדכי יונה ז״ל

A man of integrity and compassion

Dedicated by
*Mr. and Mrs. Merton Paul
and family*

In Loving Memory of

ר׳ יצחק אריה
ב״ר אהרן הכהן ז״ל

ומרת צביה
בת ר׳ בערל ע״ה

Dedicated by their daughter
*Mrs. A. Barclay
and granddaughter Elaine*

May the learning of this ספר be a זכות
for our beloved mother

מרת חיה בת פסח ע"ה

נפטרה אחרון של פסח תשס"ב

Dedicated by the Sherwood family

ת.נ.צ.ב.ה.

In honor of Rav Elozor Barclay, an outstanding
Moreh Halacha who devotedly and clearly
transmitted to us the details of halacha
so vital to our lives.

In the zechus of his harbatzas Torah over the years,
may the רבש"ע give him and his rebbitzen
much b'racha and continued Yiddishe nachas
from their children and grandchildren.

In appreciation,
The Talmidos of his Neveh Yaakov
Evening Halacha Shiur

לע"נ

ר' דוד בן ר' אהרן זצ"ל

מרת דרשנא בת ר' נחמן ע"ה

הונצח ע"י משפחתם

ת.נ.צ.ב.ה.

לע"נ

מרת מלכה בת ר' נתן הלוי ע"ה

נפטרה י' תמוז תשס"ב

הונצח ע"י משפחות גודוויין וספייער

ת.נ.צ.ב.ה.

לע"נ

מרת יהודית בת ר' צבי ע"ה
(Edith Margulies)

נפטרה כ"ה טבת תשס"ב

הונצח ע"י משפחתה

ת.נ.צ.ב.ה.

לע"נ

מרת בלומה בת ר' שמואל ע"ה

אשה יראת ה' היא תתהלל

ת.נ.צ.ב.ה.

נדבת משפחתה